SANDRA FOX

RAPID WEIGHT LOSS FOR BEGINNERS

**The New Complete Cookbook and Diet Guide.
Meal Prep Magazine Program for Quick
Weight Loss Success with Point System.
Slow Cooker Recipes.
(Crockpot)**

Riverhead Free Library
330 Court Street
Riverhead NY 11901

Additionally, the information in the following pages is intended only for informational purposes and should thus be thought of as universal. As befitting its nature, it is presented without assurance regarding its prolonged validity or interim quality. Trademarks that are mentioned are done without written consent and can in no way be considered an endorsement from the trademark holder.

Table of Contents

INTRODUCTION 13

WHAT TO KNOW BEFORE STARTING A RAPID WEIGHT LOSSPROGRAM 20

CHAPTER 1: RAPID WEIGHT LOSS WITH POINT SYSTEMS 30

EVERYTHING YOU NEED TO KNOW ABOUT FREESTYLE POINTS 38

CHAPTER 2: BREAKFAST RECIPES 58

BACON EGG MUFFINS 58

BROCCOLI EGG MUFFINS..61

PEANUT BUTTER OATS 64

BREAKFAST CASSEROLE 66

CHEESE BASIL FRITTATA...67

TOMATO SALMON MORNING...69

CHAPTER 3: FREESTYLE SOUPS AND STEWS 72

STEAK BEAN SOUP 72

CHICKEN CORN SPINACH SOUP..74

TOMATO HERB SOUP..77

POTATO BEAN STEW...78

CHICKEN MUSHROOM SOUP 80

TURKEY GREEN BEAN SOUP 82

GINGER CARROT SOUP 83

CHICKEN BRUSSELS SOUP 85

CHAPTER 4: FREESTYLE CHICKED AND POULTRY 89

MEXICAN BEAN CHICKEN 89

CHEESE CREAM CHICKEN 91

CHICKEN VEGGIE RICE 98

TURKEY APPLE PATTIES 99

MARINARA CHEESE CHICKEN 104

TURKEY BEAN CHILI 105

ORANGE PINEAPPLE CHICKEN 107

BBQ TURKEY MEATBALLS 109

CHICKEN MUSHROOM MEATBALLS 111

TURKEY VEGETABLE MIX 116

CHAPTER 5: FREESTYLE RED MEAT 122

ZUCCHINI CHILI BEEF 122

BEEF LETTUCE BURGERS 124

CREAMUY PORK CHOPS 126

BEEF BROCOLI DINNER 128

ROAST TACE WRAPS 130

GRILLED SPICED CHOPS 133

CHAPTER 6: FREESTYLE FISH AND SEAFOOD 137

AVOCADO CRAB SALAD 137

POTATO MAYO FISH 138

TUNA CRANBERRY SALAD 143

SALMON ASPARAGUS TREAT 145

BAKED SPICED FISH 147

COD SHRIMP STEW 150

SHRIMP BLUE CHEESE SALAD 152

CHAPTER 7: FREESTYLE MEATLESS RECIPES 156

MANGO ARUGULA SALAD 156

CREAM MAYO CORN 159

EGGS GREEN BEAN SALAD 160

FETA CHICKPEA SALAD 161

FETA CORN TREAT 165

MARINARA BROCCOLI MEAL 165

ARUGULA GREENS SALAD 167

EGG MAYO SALAD 170

CHAPTER 8: FREESTYLE DESSERTS 173

BLUEBERRY LEMON MUFFINS...173

APPLESAUCE BEAN BROWNIES 177

PUMPKIN CAKE MUFFINS...179

CHAPTER 9: BASICS OF RAPID WEIGHT LOSS 183

CHAPTER 10: ADVANTAGES AND DISADVANTAGES OF
RAPID WEIGHT LOSS...192

CHAPTER 11: WHY RAPID WEIGHT LOSS LEAVES YOU
FEELING LIKE A DISAPPOINTMENT...205

CONCLUSION 215

INTRODUCTION

Rapid weight loss is a well-known diet that assists individuals with shedding pounds through its point-checking framework. You're required to follow your nourishment admission (as every nourishment has a doled-out point worth) and remain inside your day by day focuses spending plan. Since unhealthy or void calorie nourishments utilize more focuses, constraining those will decrease your general vitality admission and assist you with shedding pounds.

This doesn't mean the arrangement is the correct decision for everybody, however. While Rapid weight loss has its positive characteristics, it additionally may prompt unfortunate dieting propensities. A few people feel the steady following is disagreeable, and others may control focuses, (for example, skipping dinners to bank focuses for less solid nourishments). It likewise can be exorbitant after some time.

Adjusted and Flexible

Rapid weight loss offers one of the most adaptable business diets available. By relegating vegetables, natural products, and lean proteins an estimation of zero points, the diet urges you to make these the heft of your suppers while as yet taking into consideration sufficient grains and dairy inside your day by day Points assignment.

Shows Lifelong Skills

Regardless of what diet plan you pick, you need it to be something you can pursue forever. Rapid weight loss shows basic good dieting abilities that will work well for you after some time - like estimating your segments and serving sizes and urging you to cook nourishment at home.

No Foods are Forbidden

There is no rundown of nourishments to stay away from on Rapid weight loss like you'll discover on different diets. Rather, you'll tally Points and gain Points. The point framework urges you to eat well nourishment yet in addition enables you to enjoy with sweet treats or snacks every so often.

Gradual Weight Loss

You can hope to lose one to two pounds every week on Rapid weight loss. A few studies have bolstered these cases and demonstrated the program to be viable for weight misfortune.

For instance, one investigation distributed in 2017 in Lancet thought about weight misfortune among those utilizing self-improvement materials, Rapid weight loss for 12 weeks, or Rapid weight loss for 52 weeks. The 52-week program prompted preferable outcomes over the 12-week program, and the 12-week program would be advised to results than the independently directed program.

Another 2015 efficient survey in Annals of inner drug analyzed a few business weight misfortune programs. The examination found that those on Rapid weight loss lost 2.6 percent more weight contrasted with control groups.

Strangely, a far reaching influence may likewise exist for companions of those taking an interest in Rapid weight loss (or other weight misfortune programs). A study distributed in 2018 in Obesity discovered significant weight misfortune among life partners of those taking an interest in Rapid weight loss, despite the fact that they themselves didn't join.

Huge amounts of Support and Resources

Rapid weight loss offers a greater number of assets than most other diet programs. You'll discover the application and site convenient for figuring and following Points, just as discovering formula thoughts.

If you like responsibility and gathering support, you can likewise go to the ordinary gathering gatherings. You can even pursue a superior participation that incorporates customized instructing for one-on-one help.

Additionally, if you possess a Fitbit for weight misfortune, or utilize another gadget or weight misfortune application like Jawbone, Withings, Misfit, Garmin Vivofit, Apple Health, or Map-My-Run, you can synchronize your action to Rapid weight loss. This encourages you deal with all your physical movement and weight misfortune information in one spot.

Diminishes Diabetes Risk

Because Rapid weight loss steers clients towards nutritious choices and assists individuals with getting in shape, the program has been related with a decreased danger of type 2 diabetes or better glucose control among those with diabetes.

For instance, an examination distributed in 2017 in BMJ open diabetes inquire about and care took a gander at the impacts of alluding those with pre-diabetes to a free Rapid weight loss program. The individuals who took part shed pounds and diminished hemoglobin A1c levels (a proportion of glucose control). Truth be told, 38 percent of patients came back to totally typical blood glucose metrics.

Different studies have discovered comparative outcomes among those with pre-diabetes, incorporating a study distributed in BMJ Open Diabetes Research and Care in 2017. Another study distributed in 2016 in Obesity (Silver Springs) has likewise indicated the individuals who as of now have diabetes experienced weight misfortune and better glucose control when following the Rapid weight loss program.

Advances Exercise

The Rapid weight loss framework energizes a lot of day by day development and exercise. You procure Points with development that assist you with offsetting your nourishment admission. Direction is accommodated new exercisers and for the individuals who can work out more enthusiastically and consume more calories.

Despite the fact that there are numerous advantages to Rapid weight loss, that doesn't mean it's an ideal choice for everybody. Think about the downsides before putting resources into the arrangement.

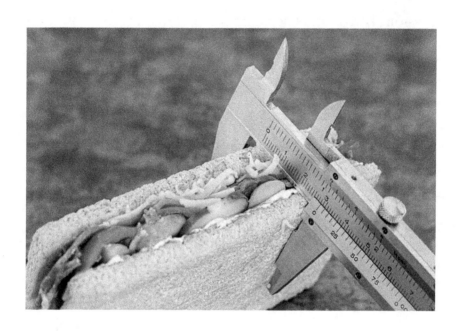

WHAT TO KNOW BEFORE STARTING A RAPID WEIGHT LOSSPROGRAM

When it comes to weight reduction, most specialists concur a solid eating routine is more powerful than work out. Individuals often work out to an ever-increasing extent, urgently trusting they can eat anything they desire. Yet, it's a decent diet that has the genuine effect with your waistline.

That is the reason individuals who effectively get thinner — and keep it off — receive lifelong, smart dieting propensities.

"I wish I hadn't attempted every one of the contrivances and burned through a great many dollars on prevailing fashion counts calories that never worked," Heather Crockett Oram told TODAY, by means of email. Oram shed 82 pounds by changing her eating and exercise propensities. "I wish somebody would have revealed to me it is anything but a win or bust kind of thing."

Oram and nine other ladies share what they wished they knew before changing their weight control plans.

1. It's OK to fall flat.

When individuals initially receive smart dieting propensities, they here and there figure they can never eat a cut of cake or a bit of pizza. Then when they do, they feel like disappointments. Be that as it may, individuals who succeed realize one mix-up isn't the apocalypse.

"The occasions when ... my treat day transformed into a treat month, I wish I had somebody to reveal to me that it is OK and simply refocus," Patricia Wilson told TODAY. Wilson shed 100 pounds.

"It is OK to fizzle," she said by means of email. "For whatever length of time that you flop forward — don't surrender, continue pushing through."

2. Eating well sets aside cash.

LeAnne Manuel thought purchasing solid foods cost more cash. That was one of her reasons to eat prepared and low quality nourishments. In any case, not long after subsequent to changing her dietary patterns, she learned she was sparing dollars.

"We really spend much less at this point. For one, the measure of ingredients has curtailed. I eat about a large portion of the volume that I used to eat," said Manuel, who shed 165 pounds.

3. Rolling out little improvements has a major sway.

In the past when Jenna Winchester had a go at getting more fit, she cut every single terrible food from her eating regimen without a moment's delay. This made weight reduction testing because she longed for such a large number of undesirable foods simultaneously and felt overpowered.

Be that as it may, when she began her ongoing effective weight reduction venture, which prompted a 210-pound misfortune, she did it with little changes.

"Begin little. Try not to go insane and cut out each and every awful food at the same time. Begin by removing a certain something, similar to pop or desserts, and afterward gradually add on to that," Winchester said.

4. You feel the progressions right away.

Subsequent to practicing with a coach for a month and shedding 17 pounds, Lydia Dziubanek chose to present lean protein, foods grown from the ground into her eating regimen. She started getting in shape snappier, however she likewise was stunned by how she felt.

"Changing my eating regimen brought numerous shocks, however most significant was the acknowledgment of how much better I felt once introductory migraines left from my body breaking free of the sugar yearnings. I felt lighter and increasingly lively," she told TODAY

5. Sound diets incorporate including not simply subtracting.

When Jordan Kohanim once thought of diets, she thought she needed to limit what she ate. During her 70-pound weight reduction, she understood she could include foods and still get more fit.

"I included more foods grown from the ground," she said. "Cause yourself to eat two cups of veggies before you eat that sandwich."

When she included increasingly nutritious foods, she discovered her longings for unfortunate foods vanished.

6. Food is fuel.

When Amy-Jo Reid originally began getting thinner, she figured she could just have protein shakes or chicken bosom. Yet, then somebody offered her some guidance and eating turned out to be additionally energizing — and satisfying.

"Somebody instructed me to begin taking a gander at food as 'fuel for my body.' That was a gigantic assistance," she said. "Blend it up and attempt new foods. You will be astounded."

7. Focus on enthusiastic changes.

In the same way as other individuals, Dziubanek ate when her mind-sets shifted. It took some time for her to understand that she utilized food to alleviate her feelings.

"Concentrate on changing your dietary patterns when you get focused, furious, or praising," she said. "We as a whole battle with food."

8. Sound food is really delectable.

Following quite a while of noshing on greasy and sugary foods, Brittany Horton figured changing her eating routine would mean she could just eat tasteless, exhausting foods over and over. However, Horton, who shed 208 pounds, learned she wasn't right.

"Sound food really tasted great," she said. "I altogether appreciate the assortment, all things considered,

"I began on a 1,500-calorie diet and it was amazing what you could really expend as opposed to eating low quality nourishment," she said.

9. Segment size issues.

When Manuel began seeing her part measures, she understood she was eating a few times what she ought to be. Estimating her dinners helped her shed pounds.

"There is no speculating with segment size, so purchase a food scale to assist you with arriving at your objectives," she said. "Indeed, even now, about three years into my adventure, my speculations are off when it comes to segment size."

10. Be inventive!

Like Reid, Young immediately became exhausted with eating something very similar for each dinner. That is when she understood she expected to grow her go-to plans.

"Ensure that you have an assortment of plans because eating something very similar arranged a similar way can get exhausting," she said. "Pinterest works for me."

11. It is anything but an eating routine

"Diets are intended to end and significantly after you lose the weight, your adventure never stops," said Reid. "The battle never stops."

Where do I start if I need to get thinner?" I think I have heard this inquiry multiple times over my most recent 10 years in the wellness business. While everybody's outline for weight reduction will (and should) be different, there are unquestionably sure beginning obstructs that work for totally everybody.

You're not the only one if you don't have the foggiest idea where to begin. There are huge amounts of individuals simply like you and you ought not feel embarrassed or humiliated to pose this inquiry. Be that as it may, ideally this posting will respond to this inquiry and you won't have to pose to it any longer – that is my objective!

1. Choose!

This is the #1 most significant thing ever. YOU need to conclude that you're tired of the manner in which you've been living and it's the ideal opportunity for a change. YOU need to hit that point – nobody will have the option to constrain you to do it. YOU need to place in the work each day, so this dedication and choice need to originate from YOU!

I've worked with individuals before who hadn't completely chosen however enlisted me as a mentor at any rate. It was extremely evident because the drive, assurance and any flash were gone rapidly. Truth be told, many even misled me about what they were eating or would conceal it from me when I would go into the room! Gee... .this is for YOU (not me!). It totally must be for YOU!

2. Take A WALK

Strolling has unbelievable advantages and you can do it whenever, anyplace.

Strolling is a low-stress, low-sway type of activity (in contrast to running and hopping) and is an amazing fat killer. Simply ribbon up your strolling shoes, running shoes, preparing shoes (whatever!) and go! This is the ideal time to tune in to persuasive digital recordings, your preferred playlist or a book recording.

Try not to think, simply walk!

3. Make A VISION BOARD

Experience a lot of magazines and cut out photos of your fantasy life, body, outlook, house, and so forth. Put everything on a plug or publication barricade and balance it in a spot that you'll see each day. See it, imagine what it feels like to arrive at those objectives (truly, you can close your eyes) and DECIDE that you will arrive regardless.

I have a great deal of pictures of Oprah Winfrey and Jillian Michaels on my vision board. Also, I often contact their heart and afterward contact mine – as though to move the core of these individuals who rouse me to myself. I couldn't care less if that sounds bizarre, I do that and it's stunning!

4. Try not to DRINK YOUR CALORIES – WATER ONLY!

No juices, no pop, no games drinks... simply water!

Goodness and no eating regimen pop. The artificial sugars still enact the "compensate pathways" that are initiated when we eat sweet foods. In any case, there are no calories in them so there is nothing to kill that switch – in this manner bringing about increasingly more undesirable food desires.

Go for 35-40 ml for each kg of body weight. Also, include 500-1000 ml for each hour of activity.

CHAPTER 1: Rapid Weight Loss with Point Systems

No nourishment is taboo when you pursue this arrangement, which doesn't make you purchase any prepackaged suppers.

Rapid Weight Loss appoints different nourishments a Point esteem. Nutritious nourishments that top you off have less focuses than garbage with void calories. The eating plan factors sugar, fat, and protein into its focuses counts to direct you toward natural products, veggies, and lean protein, and away from stuff that is high in sugar and immersed fat.

You'll have a Point focus on that is set up dependent on your body and objectives. For whatever length of time that you remain inside your everyday target, you can spend those Points anyway you'd like, even on liquor or treat, or spare them to utilize one more day.

However, more beneficial, lower-calorie nourishments cost less focuses. Furthermore, a few things presently have o points.

Level of Effort: Medium

Rapid Weight Loss is intended to make it simpler to change your propensities long haul, and it's adaptable enough that you ought to have the option to adjust it to your life. You'll change your eating and lifestyle designs - a considerable lot of which you may have had for quite a long time - and you'll make new ones.

How much exertion it takes relies upon the amount you'll need to change your propensities.

Cooking and shopping: Expect to figure out how to shop, cook solid nourishments, and eat out in manners that help your weight loss objective without holding back on taste or expecting to purchase strange nourishments.

Bundled nourishments or dinners: Not required.

In-person gatherings: Optional.

Exercise: You'll get a customized action objective and access to the program's application that tracks Points. You get acknowledgment for the entirety of your action.

Does It Allow for Dietary Restrictions or Preferences?

Because you pick how you spend your Points, you can at present do Rapid Weight Loss if you're a veggie lover, vegetarian, have different inclinations, or if you have to confine salt or fat.

What Else You Should Know

Cost: Rapid Weight Loss offers three plans: Online just, online with gatherings, or online with one-on-one training through telephone calls and messages. Check the Rapid Weight Loss site for the evaluating for the online-just and online-with gatherings alternatives (you'll have to enter your ZIP code).

Costs and offers may differ.

Backing: Besides the discretionary in-person gatherings (presently called health workshops) and individual instructing, Rapid Weight Loss Program has an application, online network, a magazine, and a site with plans, tips, examples of overcoming adversity, and that's only the tip of the iceberg.

Does It Work?

Rapid Weight Loss is one of the well-looked into weight loss programs accessible. What's more, indeed, it works.

Numerous studies have demonstrated that the arrangement can assist you with getting more fit and keep it off.

For example, an investigation from The American Journal of Medicine demonstrated that individuals doing Rapid Weight Loss lost more weight than those attempting to drop beats without anyone else.

Rapid Weight Loss positioned first both for "Best Weight Loss Diet" and for "Best Commercial Diet Plan" in the 2018 rankings from U.S. News and World Report.

Generally speaking, it's a great, simple to-pursue program.

Is It Good for Certain Conditions?

Rapid Weight Loss is useful for anybody. In any case, its attention on nutritious, low-calorie nourishments makes it extraordinary for individuals with hypertension, elevated cholesterol, diabetes, and even coronary illness.

If you pick any premade dinners, check the names, as some might be high in sodium.

Work with your primary care physician so they can check your advancement, as well. This is particularly significant for individuals with diabetes, as you may need to alter your medication as you get in shape.

If the idea of gauging your nourishment or checking calories make your head turn, this is a perfect program because it takes every necessary step for you. The online instrument allocates a specific number an incentive to every nourishment, even eatery nourishments, to make it simple to remain on track.

If you don't have the foggiest idea about your way around the kitchen, the premade dinners and bites make it simple. They're a speedy and simple approach to control partition sizes and calories.

You don't need to drop any nourishment from your eating routine, yet you should constrain divide sizes to curtail calories.

The accentuation on foods grown from the ground implies the eating routine is high in fiber, which helps keep you full. Also, the program is easy to pursue, making it simpler to adhere to. You can likewise discover Rapid Weight Loss Program premade dinners at your neighborhood market.

A major favorable position of Rapid Weight Loss is their site. They offer exhaustive data on abstaining from excessive food intake, exercise, cooking, and wellness tips, just as online care groups.

Be set up to go through some cash to get the full advantages of the vigorous program. It tends to be somewhat expensive, yet it's well justified, despite all the trouble to harvest the wellbeing advantages of getting more fit and keeping it off.

Part Benefits

Dieters who join Rapid weight loss are known as "individuals."

Individuals can browse a few projects with differing levels of help.

An essential online program incorporates every minute of every day online visit support, just as applications and different instruments. Individuals can pay more for face to face bunch gatherings or one-on-one help from a Rapid weight loss individual mentor.

Individuals additionally get access to an online database of thousands of nourishments and plans, notwithstanding a following application for logging Points.

Also, Rapid weight loss supports physical action by relegating a wellness objective utilizing Points.

Every action can be signed into the Rapid weight loss application until the client arrives at their week after week FitPoint objective.

Exercises like moving, strolling and cleaning would all be able to be tallied towards your Point objective.

Rapid weight loss additionally gives wellness recordings and exercise schedules for their individuals.

Alongside diet and exercise directing, Rapid weight loss sells bundled nourishment like solidified suppers, cereal, chocolates and low-calorie dessert.

Outline

Rapid weight loss doles out guide esteems toward nourishments. Individuals must remain under their assigned day by day nourishment and drink focuses to meet their weight-misfortune objectives.

Would it be able to Help You Lose Weight?

Rapid weight loss utilizes a science-based way to deal with weight misfortune, accentuating the significance of part control, nourishment decisions and moderate, predictable weight misfortune.

Dissimilar to numerous craze diets that guarantee unreasonable outcomes over brief timeframes, Rapid weight loss discloses to individuals that they ought to hope to lose .5 to 2 pounds (.23 to .9 kg) every week.

The program features lifestyle modification and advice individuals on the best way to settle on better choices by utilizing the Points framework, which organizes sound nourishments.

Numerous studies have demonstrated that Rapid weight loss can help with weight misfortune.

Truth be told, Rapid weight loss gives a whole page of their site to scientific examinations supporting their program.

One study found that overweight individuals who were advised to get more fit by their PCPs lost twice as a lot of weight on the Rapid weight loss program than the individuals who got standard weight misfortune directing from an essential care proficient.

In spite of the fact that this investigation was subsidized by Rapid weight loss, information gathering and examination were facilitated by a free research group.

Besides, an audit of 39 controlled examinations found that members following the Rapid weight loss program lost 2.6% more weight than members who got different sorts of guiding.

Another controlled investigation in more than 1,200 hefty grown-ups found that members who pursued the Rapid weight loss program for one year lost significantly more weight than the individuals who got self-improvement materials or brief weight-misfortune counsel.

In addition, members following Rapid weight loss for one year were increasingly fruitful at keeping up their weight misfortune more than two years, contrasted with different gatherings.

Rapid weight loss is one of only a handful scarcely any weight-misfortune programs with demonstrated outcomes from randomized controlled preliminaries, which are considered the "best quality level" of therapeutic research.

EVERYTHING YOU NEED TO KNOW ABOUT FREESTYLE POINTS

My mom had done Rapid weight loss when I was growing up, so I was super familiar with the process. When she was feeling unhealthy, she always lamented that she needed "to get back on Rapid weight loss," as if it was the only way she'd feel better.

So, with my mom's ringing endorsement — along with tons of others — I began Rapid weight loss in the summer of 2017. And to my absolute shock, it worked. In about a year, I dropped 60 pounds, 50 of which came off in about nine months.

It hasn't always been easy and, even with my mom to guide me, the program, especially with its changes, can be daunting at first. I wish I had known few things going in, so I'm here to impart this wisdom onto you.

Just a note that everyone's experience will be different — this is just mine. When it comes to weight loss, you have to do what is best for you and what is advised by your doctor.

Get the tools, but don't go overboard.

The awesome and the intimidating thing about Rapid weight loss is you have to figure out what's right for you. Nothing is off limits, and nothing is required. But, it can help to be stocked up with a few key tools before you go in.

A food scale to measure meat, for example, helps you figure out the exact points of your meal, which keeps you from eating too little or too much. Meal prep containers are essential to storing big batches of healthy, homemade treats. Similarly, keeping low-point foods — like PB2 powder, Kodiak Cakes, Western Bagels, Quaker Oatmeal Packets, cans of tuna, beef jerky — on hand helps when you need a quick fix.

That said, you don't need to blow your paycheck on stuff you may not use. Start by replacing some common pantry items with lower-point equivalents. Start fresh, but start slow.

Read up on the more confusing elements.

Like any diet, there can be some things about Rapid weight loss that you may screw up if you don't know better. For instance, fruit is zero points but if you put it in a smoothie, it becomes a point-filled food. Eat one piece of bread during breakfast and one during dinner, and it could be fewer points than if you ate them together.

Some of this will honestly be trial and error, but talking to other members about their experiences and reading up as much as you can is your best defense against rookie mistakes.

Get some support.

I personally don't go to Rapid weight loss meetings because, if "Sex and the City" is to be believed, I'll meet a man, eat half a Krispy Kreme donut with him, and then break his heart because of differences in the bedroom. Actually, I'm mostly just scared of people.

Tons of people find so much joy and support in weekly meetings. If that sounds like you, I urge you to give it a shot. If you're more like me, though, there are lots of online resources that give you the same sense of community.

The "connect" social network on the Rapid weight loss app is a great way to ask any questions you might have and share funny anecdotes and photos during your journey. You can also use Instagram to connect, and even find recipes, tips, and tricks from like-minded people who want you to succeed. (I actually got myself a finstagram just for my weight loss stuff and I'd highly recommend it.)

Something that people don't tell you before you start this program is that weight loss and a healthy lifestyle are amazing, but it can also feel incredibly isolating. Having that support from people who get it is validating. And it will keep you from talking your partner's ear off if they're not on the program with you.

Figure out meals you can eat a million times without becoming bored.

I've realized that I can eat one of two different breakfasts every day and not get bored. Mine are oatmeal, fruit, and non-fat Greek yogurt or an English muffin with a hard-boiled egg, Laughing Cow cheese, and hot sauce.

Knowing that I have one meal out of the day figured out frees my brain up to think of lunches and dinners. Plus, knowing I have one meal planned keeps me from reaching for sugary treat when I'm hungry.

When in doubt, simple is best.

People on Rapid weight loss are honestly the MacGyvers of diets. They can find a way to make any kind of comfort food light and plan-friendly, and I've had a blast making lighter banana bread, enchiladas, mac and cheese, and more.

But sometimes, trying these recipes can get overwhelming and, personally, my body doesn't react well to tons of dairy or carbs, whether it's full-fat or not.

When in doubt, it's best to keep it simple — lean proteins and veggies are your friends. I always have chicken breasts and some kind of frozen veggie in the freezer because that will likely be lower in points than any kind of concoction I try to cook.

Comparison is the thief of joy.

Remember that community of people I mentioned before? It's a double-edge sword.

My first week on Rapid weight loss, I felt like such a badass. I had been tracking and measuring to a tee and I was so motivated. Then I got on the scale on my weigh-in day and ... nothing. I had been working out and eating well all week for what felt like nothing.

Being on Instagram and seeing everyone dropping four pounds in a week while I had nothing to show for it sucked. I was baffled why I hadn't lost weight right away.

But I quickly realized, thanks to that same community, that everyone's body is different. I would go on to have those four-pound weight loss weeks and I would go on to have weeks where I'd gain two pounds. So did those people I was comparing myself to.

If you sit there and agonize over what other people are losing, you'll get nowhere. Their body is not your body and your progress isn't theirs. What you probably don't see are the weeks that they don't lose either and the nights they go HAM on some queso and chips. Don't worry about how the plan is working for others — focus on you!

Track your "splurge" meals.

The biggest mistake I made when starting Rapid weight loss was giving up on weekends. I would just assume I used all of my "weekly points" on some take out on Friday night and call it a day without tracking it. But because I didn't track it, I would still see those weekly points there, and then feel OK to eat a bagel with brunch on Saturday. And a mimosa. And some bacon.

That's not how it's supposed to work. You should totally feel free to use your weeklies (seriously, use them!), but you should also be tracking everything if you want to be on the program — even if it wipes out all your weeklies and then some. Otherwise, you'll trick yourself into thinking you have more wiggle room than you think.

I am all for taking a few days off for vacations, holidays, or your own wellbeing. But in "normal weeks" track those points, even if it stings.

Try not to sweat the small stuff.

I've spent my fair share of time crying on the scale, despairing out over a meal that ended up being triple the points I planned, or agonizing because the only option at lunch was least 30 points.

Somehow I am still here to tell the tale.

Everything seems incredibly catastrophic and important at the time, but honestly, life sometimes gets in the way of your eating plan. It can feel so upsetting when you know you've worked so hard only to see your progress sabotaged by a rogue cookie craving.

But it's also important to remember that, although we often say life is short, it's also very long. You were put on earth to do more than lose weight and ultimately, that late-night ice cream with your partner may be worth the splurge.

While no one wants to have roadblocks, sometimes life gets in the way. The important thing is not to let a roadblock derail you completely. It's imperative that you accept your lumps and move on ASAP. After all, consistent, slow weight loss and weight management is the way to go. And if you're truly in this for the long haul, you're going to hit some bumps

RAPID WEIGHT LOSS FREESTYLE: FOOD TO EAT

If yearning is your center name and holder tails you like the plague, your diet might be feeling the loss of the Ingredients that convey reasonable vitality and help keep enormous cravings under control. An indication is feeling covetous when your Points Budget is close as far as possible. For a quick fix, start eating the nourishments that can assist you with feeling full more—so you go through your days feeling fulfilled, not starving.

Here are six science-upheld picks to add all the more fortitude to your suppers and tidbits:

1. Cereal

Imminent transient studies propose cereal utilization assists lower with bodying mass list and body weight. Why? One reason is that oats are wealthy in dissolvable fiber, a kind of fiber that becomes thick and gel-like when joined with fluid, says Wendy Bazilian, DrPH, RD, coauthor of Eat Clean, Stay Lean: The Diet and proprietor of Bazilian's Health in San Diego. The oats are thought to affect hunger decreasing hormones which makes it almost certain you'll eat less, and they void out of your stomach at a more slow rate than basic carbs, for example, found in a donut for instance.

Be that as it may, there's one significant proviso: Because dissolvable fiber needs fluid to thicken up, oats appear to be the most filling when they're cooked in water or milk to make cereal. "A biscuit or breakfast bar made with oats most likely won't have a similar degree of impact, since they don't have as a lot of water," Bazilian says.

2. Beans

Prepare them into plate of mixed greens, use them in soup, or puree them into a plunge. Including beans and vegetables like chickpeas, dark beans, and lentils to a dinner expands satiety by a normal of 31%, as indicated by an ongoing scientific audit distributed in the diary Obesity.

When it comes to completion, these little powerhouses appear to pack a one-two punch. They are perplexing sugars, which convey vitality and they are wealthy in fiber. Be that as it may, they likewise have protein, which takes more time to process — which causes you remain fulfilled for more. "It's a moderate, supported arrival of glucose, which can lengthen satiety," Bazilian says.

3. Non-bland vegetables

Veggies like verdant greens, broccoli, cauliflower, asparagus, peppers, and celery have low calorie thickness. That implies that they're low in calories for their serving size—but since they're high in water and fiber, they have more volume which means they occupy more room in your stomach. "If you pick nourishments that have a lower thickness of calories in each chomp, you'll get a greater bit for your calorie needs," says

Barbara Rolls, PhD, Director of the Laboratory for the Study of Human Ingestive Behavior at Penn State University and creator of The Ultimate Volumetrics Diet.

A valid example: You'd need to eat multiple cups of cooked infant spinach to devour 100 calories, however you'd get a similar measure of calories from only 1 measly tablespoon of margarine. Which one do you think would top you off additional?

4. Eggs

Have them in the first part of the day, and you very well might feel more full throughout the day. One study found that ladies who were overweight detailed that they devoured less nourishment for as long as 36 hours when they had eggs for breakfast, contrasted with when they ate bagels. (Discussion about mind blowing, right?)

That could be because eggs are pressed with protein—which condensations at a more slow rate than starch based nourishments which helps keep you fulfilled longer, says Bazilian. (A huge egg conveys 6g protein.) But that is not all. A little report likewise recommends that eggs could stifle the creation of the craving hormone ghrelin, which could help nix the desire to nosh.

5. Greek yogurt

A cup of Greek yogurt conveys around 22g protein, which will help diminish the craving to eat and keep you feeling full for more. In addition, it's generally high in water, so it includes volume in your stomach. Consolidated, those two things will keep you fulfilled, Bazilian says.

Obviously, not all yogurts are made equivalent. Plain yogurt is a superior decision than the seasoned stuff, since it's free of included sugars which, in abundance, have been connected to expanded chance for sickness.

6. Brothy soup

Beginning with a soup can help check calorie admission at supper time, a few studies appear. Like non-dull vegetables, soups have a low-calorie thickness—all that fluid will help top you off for generally not many calories, Rolls says.

The key is staying with juices or tomato-based soups rather than cream-based ones. Think minestrone or butternut squash. For much all the more backbone—like if you're having soup for a dinner—consider including a wellspring of lean protein like destroyed chicken, Rolls says.

RAPID WEIGHT LOSS DIET: RESTRICTED FOOD

The nourishments you eat can majorly affect your weight.

A few nourishments, similar to full-fat yogurt, coconut oil and eggs, help with weight misfortune.

Different nourishments, particularly prepared and refined items, can make you put on weight.

Here are 11 nourishments to evade when you're attempting to get more fit.

1. French Fries and Potato Chips

Entire potatoes are sound and filling, however french fries and potato chips are definitely not. They are high in calories, and it's anything but difficult to eat an excessive number of them.

In observational investigations, expending French fries and potato chips has been connected to weight gain.

One concentrate even found that potato chips may add to more weight gain per serving than some other nourishment.

In addition, prepared, cooked or singed potatoes may contain malignant growth causing substances called acrylamides. Thusly, it's ideal to eat plain, bubbled potatoes.

2. Sugary Drinks

Sugar-improved drinks, similar to pop, are one of the unhealthiest nourishments on earth.

They are emphatically connected with weight gain and can have grievous wellbeing impacts when devoured in abundance.

Despite the fact that sugary beverages contain a ton of calories, your mind doesn't enroll them like strong nourishment.

Fluid sugar calories don't make you feel full, and you won't eat less nourishment to redress. Rather, you wind up including these calories top of your ordinary admission.

If you are not kidding about getting thinner, consider surrendering sugary beverages totally.

3. White Bread

White bread is profoundly refined and often contains a ton of included sugar.

It is high on the glycemic list and can spike your glucose levels.

One investigation of 9,267 individuals found that eating two cuts (120 grams) of white bread every day was connected to a 40% more serious danger of weight addition and corpulence.

Luckily, there are numerous solid options in contrast to traditional wheat bread. One is Ezekiel bread, which is presumably the most advantageous bread available.

In any case, remember that all wheat breads do contain gluten. Some different choices incorporate oopsie bread, cornbread and almond flour bread.

4. Sweet treats

Sweet treats are very undesirable. They pack a great deal of included sugar, included oils and refined flour into a little bundle.

Sweet treats are high in calories and low in supplements. A normal estimated piece of candy shrouded in chocolate can contain around 200–300 calories, and extra-huge bars may contain much more.

Shockingly, you can discover pieces of candy all over. They are even deliberately put in stores in request to entice shoppers into getting them rashly.

If you are longing for a tidbit, eat a bit of organic product or a bunch of nuts.

Outline

Pieces of candy comprise of undesirable Ingredients like sugar, refined flour and included oils. They are high in calories, yet not very filling.

5. Most Fruit Juices

Most organic product juices you find at the general store share next to no practically speaking with entire natural product.

Organic product juices are exceptionally handled and stacked with sugar.

Truth be told, they can contain the same amount of sugar and calories as pop, if not more.

Likewise, natural product squeeze for the most part has no fiber and doesn't require biting.

This implies a glass of squeezed orange won't have indistinguishable consequences for completion from an orange, making it simple to expend enormous amounts in a short measure of time.

Avoid organic product squeeze and eat entire natural product.

6. Baked goods, Cookies and Cakes

Baked goods, cookies and cakes are stuffed with undesirable Ingredients like included sugar and refined flour.

They may likewise contain artificial trans fats, which are unsafe and connected to numerous sicknesses.

Baked goods, cookies and cakes are not fulfilling, and you will probably become hungry rapidly in the wake of eating these fatty, low-supplement nourishments.

If you're desiring something sweet, go after a bit of dull chocolate.

7. A few Types of Alcohol (Especially Beer)

Liquor gives a greater number of calories than carbs and protein, or around 7 calories for every gram.

Be that as it may, the proof for liquor and weight addition isn't clear.

Savoring liquor balance is by all accounts fine and is really connected to diminished weight gain. Overwhelming drinking, then again, is related with expanded weight gain.

The kind of liquor additionally matters. Lager can cause weight gain, however savoring wine control may really be valuable.

8. Frozen yogurt

Frozen yogurt is fantastically tasty, however exceptionally unfortunate. It is high in calories, and most types are stacked with sugar.

A little segment of frozen yogurt is fine once in a while, however the issue is that it's anything but difficult to expend enormous sums in a single sitting.

Consider making your own dessert, utilizing less sugar and more advantageous Ingredients like full-fat yogurt and natural product.

Additionally, serve yourself a little part and put the frozen yogurt away with the goal that you won't wind up eating excessively.

9. Pizza

Pizza is a well-known inexpensive food. In any case, financially made pizzas likewise happen to be undesirable.

They're amazingly high in calories and often contain unfortunate Ingredients like profoundly refined flour and prepared meat.

If you need to appreciate a cut of pizza, take a stab at making one at home utilizing more advantageous Ingredients. Hand crafted pizza sauce is likewise more advantageous, since store assortments can contain heaps of sugar.

Another choice is to search for a pizza place that makes more beneficial pizzas.

10. Unhealthy Coffee Drinks

Espresso contains a few organically dynamic substances, in particular caffeine.

These synthetic concoctions can support your digestion and increment fat consuming, in any event for the time being.

Nonetheless, the negative impacts of including unfortunate Ingredients like artificial cream and sugar exceed these constructive outcomes.

Fatty espresso beverages are quite superior to pop. They're stacked with void calories that can rise to an entire supper.

If you like espresso, it's ideal to adhere to plain, dark espresso when attempting to get in shape. Including a little cream or milk is fine as well. Simply abstain from including sugar, fatty flavors and other undesirable Ingredients.

11. Nourishments High in Added Sugar

Included sugar is most likely the most exceedingly awful thing in the cutting edge diet. Overabundance sums have been connected to the absolute most genuine maladies on the planet today.

Nourishments high in included sugar for the most part give huge amounts of void calories, however are not very filling.

Instances of nourishments that may contain enormous measures of included sugar incorporate sugary breakfast oats, granola bars and low-fat, seasoned yogurt.

You should be particularly cautious when choosing "low-fat" or "sans fat" nourishments, as makers often add loads of sugar to compensate for the flavor that is lost when the fat is evacuated.

CHAPTER 2: BREAKFAST RECIPES

BACON EGG MUFFINS

This can't be rehashed enough occasions, however DO shower or oil your biscuit tin VERY well. I had a preliminary run with these two or three days before I made what you find in the photographs, and I utilized margarine to oil because I will in general abstain from cooking splashes as much as I can. I additionally utilized thick-cut bacon because I had a couple of cuts left. That was not the best decision since it didn't fresh well overall. I additionally had moderate staying issues, however my normal measured biscuit dish are not nonstick. They are those aroused cheapies from the dollar store LOL. I figured out how to get them out yet I tore the bread base a piece. Here's my guineas pigs

Trial made with huge eggs and thick-cut bacon–which isn't the best decision

So when I did them "for reals," I separated and utilized shower and I splashed each cup until it was white!!! Had no issue getting them out. I likewise utilized medium eggs because enormous (and anything over) flooded the cup. I likewise utilized a different brand of bacon and normal, not thick cut. You can obviously do this in a Texas–huge size–biscuit skillet, then bigger eggs won't present an issue.

I will alert that you watch these firmly after around 10 minutes since the bacon will begin to get over-fresh rapidly. You need it fresh so the cup holds it's shape however not consumed.

Ingredients

for 4 servings

6 cuts bacon

6 eggs

salt, taste

pepper, taste

¼ cup destroyed cheddar (25 g)

chive, to taste

Uncommon EQUIPMENT

biscuit tin

Planning

Preheat the broiler to 400°F (200°C).

Spot the cuts of bacon in the biscuit tin, enveloping by a circle.

Heat the bacon for 10 minutes.

Expel the bacon from the broiler and spill out any overabundance oil, if wanted. Split 1 egg into every one of the cups, then sprinkle with salt, pepper, and cheddar.

Heat for an additional 10 minutes, or until the egg yolks arrive at your ideal consistency.

Run a knife around the edge of each cup to release and expel. Sprinkle with chives, if wanted.

Appreciate!

BROCCOLI EGG MUFFINS

I LOVE egg biscuits. That is to say, what is superior to having smaller than usual omelets prepared to eat each and every morning? These little folks have broccoli and cheddar in them, but at the same time's stunning that you can blend in whatever you like! I at times use turkey hotdog or chorizo, a blend of veggies (ringer peppers and asparagus, to give some examples) and different cheeses. Whatever I have in my refrigerator, fundamentally. These little folks are Broccoli Cheese Egg Muffins, and they're cracking great.

An incredible method to begin the morning because they are high in protein, taste extraordinary and fulfill me until lunch. You can make these such a significant number of different ways with whatever you have staying nearby in your icebox. Here are some different recommendations.

EGG MUFFIN VARIATIONS:

Green Eggs and Ham – Spinach, hacked scallions, and ham.

Kale – Chopped onion, and hacked crisp infant kale.

Mushrooms and Cheese – cut mushrooms and Swiss cheddar.

Or on the other hand attempt these Loaded Egg Muffins.

I normally prefer to join egg whites with entire eggs, however if you rather use egg whites, that is fine as well. Refrigerate for as long as 5 days. Microwave in 30 seconds interims until warmed through.

What's more, you can utilize milk or plain Greek yogurt, contingent upon what you have and relying upon which surface you like (clue: I LOVE the surface Greek yogurt gives). Furthermore, the Greek yogurt gives additional protein which is a spectacular method to begin the day!

The other fun thing about these little angels is they are really a unique formula in my cookbook! It's loaded up with fun, basic and totally luscious plans that are DASH diet-accommodating. Which means they are made with genuine, nutritious ingredients and stacked with herbs, flavors and ingredients that make food taste AMAZING, while at the same time being mindful with how much salt we include.

In this formula for Broccoli Cheese Egg Muffins, I give a scope of how much salt to include, that way you can choose what is directly for you and your needs/needs. I additionally included ingredients like dry mustard, onion powder and garlic powder to give the egg blend so a lot of delightfulness. I am ALWAYS a fanatic of adding flavors and herbs to plans because, well, they're delightful!

How to make Broccoli & Cheese Muffins:

1. Preheat the oven to 180 degrees (375F)

2. Cook the broccoli until tender (boil or steam) and mash with the back of a fork

3. In a bowl mix together the flour, baking powder, cooked broccoli and cheese

4. Add the chopped tomatoes, oil, beaten egg, milk and mix well

5. Spoon the mixture into a greased 12 hole muffin tin (the consistency should be a moist, sticky dough that is quite thick)

6. Bake for around 30 minutes or until golden

7. Transfer to a wire rack to cool.

Once cooled store in an air tight container in the fridge for up to 3 days and eat cold or, if we're at home, I reheat them for 30 seconds in the microwave. You can also freeze them for up to 3 months, just take them out when you need them and reheat once defrosted.

As I make these for babies and toddlers I've omitted any seasoning, so add salt and pepper or paprika, mustard powder or even some fried onion if making them for older children or adults. Alternatively you could swap the broccoli for spinach, leeks, peppers or pretty much any combination of vegetables.

PEANUT BUTTER OATS

Ingredients

1-3/4 cups water

1/8 teaspoon salt

1 cup antiquated oats

2 tablespoons rich nutty spread

2 tablespoons nectar

2 teaspoons ground flaxseed

1/2 to 1 teaspoon ground cinnamon

Cleaved apple, discretionary

Purchase Ingredients

Bearings

In a little pot, heat water and salt to the point of boiling. Mix in oats; cook 5 minutes over medium warmth, mixing sporadically. Move cereal to bowls; mix in nutty spread, nectar, flaxseed, cinnamon and, if wanted, apple. Serve right away.

Nourishment Facts

3/4 cup: 323 calories, 12g fat (2g soaked fat), 0 cholesterol, 226mg sodium, 49g starch (19g sugars, 6g fiber), 11g protein.

BERRY BANANA PANCAKES

Ingredients

1 cup entire wheat flour

1/2 cup universally handy flour

2 tablespoons sugar

2 teaspoons heating powder

1/2 teaspoon salt

1 enormous egg, gently beaten

1-1/4 cups sans fat milk

3 medium ready bananas, pounded

1 teaspoon vanilla separate

1-1/2 cups crisp or solidified blueberries

Maple syrup and cut bananas, discretionary

Headings

In an enormous bowl, join the flours, sugar, heating powder and salt. Join the egg, milk, bananas and vanilla; mix into dry ingredients just until soaked.

Pour player by 1/4 cupfuls onto a hot iron covered with cooking shower; sprinkle with blueberries. Turn when air pockets structure on top; cook until second side is brilliant darker. If wanted, present with syrup and cut bananas.

Stop alternative: Freeze cooled flapjacks between layers of waxed paper in a resealable plastic cooler pack. To utilize, place hotcakes on an ungreased heating sheet, spread with foil, and warm in a preheated 375° stove 6-10 minutes. Or on the other hand, place a heap of three hotcakes on a microwave-safe plate and microwave on high for 1-1/4 to 1-1/2 minutes or until warmed through.

BREAKFAST CASSEROLE

For those of us who don't have solidified destroyed hash tans in our pieces of the world, we have to make our own! See picture underneath for a visual.

Mesh the potatoes first on the biggest side of the grater.

Absorb your destroyed potatoes water for 5 minutes, then flush in a fine work sifter (colander) under cool running water until the water runs clear.

Press the entirety of the water out with a tea towel permit to air dry on a preparing plate or heating sheet.

Store in the cooler in ziplock cooler packs until prepared to use in your morning meal!

step by step instructions to make breakfast meal

If you don't have solidified potato hash tans, start setting up that first as referenced previously.

Then, proceed onward with your morning meal!

1. Pick on your ideal meat fillings: frankfurters, bacon, ham or a mix! If including wieners and bacon, I recommend cooking them first before adding them to your egg blend.

For a veggie lover choice, you can forget about the meat.

2. Pick on your veggie fillings: We love utilizing green chime peppers (capsicum) and seeded, ready Roma tomatoes. You can likewise include corn bits, red chime peppers (capsicum), cut mushrooms and diced zucchini.

3. Pick your cheddar: Use your preferred blend OR go with our recommendation of white cheddar with a mozzarella besting.

CHEESE BASIL FRITTATA

The ingredients you'll require

You'll just need a couple of straightforward ingredients to make this delicious formula. The accurate estimations are incorporated into the formula card underneath. Here's a review of what you'll require:

Eggs

Salt and pepper

Crisp basil

Ground parmesan cheddar

Olive oil for the container

Instructions to make basil frittata

It's so natural! Look down to the formula card for the point by point directions. Here are the fundamental steps:

Whisk together the eggs, Greek yogurt, salt, and pepper.

Blend in hacked new basil leaves and ground Parmesan.

Prepare for 20-30 minutes (contingent upon your stove) in a 400F broiler. That is it!

The most effective method to serve basil frittata

It's ideal for early lunch – it makes a bubbly, solid early lunch dish. I like to have an informal breakfast spread with this frittata, smoked salmon mousse, banana bread, and almond flour rolls.

It's likewise generally excellent as a meatless supper. When I serve it for supper, I include a basic side dish, for example, steamed broccoli or tomato plate of mixed greens.

TOMATO SALMON MORNING

Ingredients

1 salmon filet (1 inch thick, around 10 ounces)

1/4 cup finely hacked onion

1/4 cup finely hacked green pepper

2 tablespoons spread, isolated

6 eggs

1/4 cup destroyed cheddar

1/4 teaspoon pepper

1 medium tomato, discretionary

1/4 medium green pepper, discretionary

Bearings

Expel the skin and bones from the salmon; cut into 1/2-in. pieces. In a 10-in. skillet, saute the salmon, onion and green pepper in 1 tablespoon margarine. Evacuate and put in a safe spot.

In a little bowl, beat eggs. Dissolve remaining margarine in same skillet over medium warmth; include eggs. As eggs set, lift edges, giving uncooked segment a chance to stream underneath.

When the eggs are set, spoon salmon blend more than one side, then sprinkle with cheddar and pepper; overlap omelet over filling. Spread and let represent 1-1/2 minutes or until the cheddar is liquefied.

If wanted, make a tomato rose. With a little sharp knife, strip the skin in a flimsy nonstop strip, beginning from the base of the tomato. Move up firmly, skin side out, from the stem end. Fold end of strip under rose and spot on omelet. From green pepper, cut two leaves. Organize on each side of tomato rose.

CHAPTER 3: FREESTYLE SOUPS AND STEWS

STEAK BEAN SOUP

This Beef and Bean Soup formula is anything but difficult to get ready. What's more, it just shows signs of improvement the more it sits and holds up until you're prepared to eat up it. Our family has consistently appreciated cooking with beans (Bush's Beans being our top choice). Beans not just loan great flavor and surface to any dish, yet they are thoroughly filling and have numerous dietary advantages as well.

I adjusted Beef and Bean Soup from our preferred Beef and Barley Soup that I have made for around fifteen years now. I chose to supplant the grain with white beans since white beans can include a similar sort of smoothness to dishes like what grain will in general give the Beef and Barley Soup. Furthermore, let me simply state, it was a consummately delicious substitution. So heavenly thus fulfilling. This is without a doubt a healthy soup, ideal for those with a hunger!

Ingredients

2 ribeye steaks

1 teaspoon ground cumin

1 teaspoon garlic powder

1/2 teaspoon dried thyme

1/2 teaspoon salt

1/2 teaspoon dark pepper

1/2 onion slashed

2 15-ounce jars dark beans (I use Bush's)

2 cloves garlic slashed

1 cup hamburger stock

Guidelines

Combine dry Ingredients through dark pepper and rub onto ribeye steaks. Spot steaks into a ziptop pack and spot in the icebox to marinate in any event one hour to medium-term, liked, however should be possible just before cooking.

Warmth skillet or barbecue container over medium warmth. Sprinkle daintily with olive oil. Expel steaks from the ziptop sack and spot into the skillet or on the flame broil dish. Burn on each side for around 3-5 minutes for each side. Put in a safe spot and permit to rest as the soup is cooking.

Add onion to skillet and saute until translucent, around 3 minutes.

Empty dark beans into medium pan over medium heat. Include onion, garlic, and hamburger stock. Cook for around 10 minutes.

Cut steak into flimsy cuts or into reduced down pieces and spot into soup.

Serve warm with harsh cream and destroyed cheddar.

CHICKEN CORN SPINACH SOUP

Ingredients

2-3 tablespoons olive oil (in addition to extra)

1/2 enormous yellow onion, finely cleaved (about a cup)

2 celery ribs, finely cut and slashed (around 3/4 cup)

1 jalapeño pepper, seeded and finely minced

2 tablespoons universally handy flour

1 cup chicken juices (in addition to extra)

2 cups milk (whatever thoughtful you like, I utilized entire milk because that is the thing that I placed in my espresso!)

2 bone-in skin-on chicken bosoms (OR, skirt this progression and simply purchase a rotisserie chicken, shred that up until you have around two cups)

3 ears of new corn pieces (OR (1)one 10-oz pack of solidified sweet corn)

1-14 oz container of cream-style corn (ah-ha! the mystery fixing!)

1/2 teaspoon dried thyme

1/4 teaspoon cayenne pepper

Salt and new ground dark pepper to taste

Discretionary

Daintily cut jalapeño to embellish

Finely hacked parsley to decorate

Slashed Green Chile*

Broil the chicken

Preheat your broiler to 400°. Pat the chicken dry with paper towels and afterward generously season both side with salt and pepper, or any flavoring blend you may like. Spot the chicken on a rimmed preparing sheet (canvassed in foil for simple tidy up) and sprinkle with a touch of olive oil. Spot this into the stove (top rack) for 35 minutes. Expel from the stove and put aside until it is cool enough to deal with. When you can, evacuate the chicken skin and bones, and shred the chicken into reduced down pieces.

While the chicken is simmering

Warmth a few tablespoons of olive oil (enough to cover the base) in a huge soup pot or Dutch stove over medium - medium high warmth. Include onion, celery and jalapeño; mix and cook for around ten minutes, or until delicate. Add a touch of salt to help this along. Include the flour, and mix and cook one more moment. Mix in the milk and stock, and keep cooking and blending until the soup starts to thicken, around 5 minutes. Then include the jar of cream style corn, thyme, cayenne pepper, mix to consolidate. Include the destroyed chicken and pack of solidified corn, and let this cook until the chicken and corn are warmed through. Taste for flavoring, and include an additional sprinkle of stock if the soup appears to be excessively thick.

Present with daintily cut jalapeño to embellish, or only a sprinkle of parsley - or both!

Far superior extra, you can solidify the rest of as long as a month and fulfill yourself after all other options have been exhausted. Shock! Lunch anticipates in your cooler.

TOMATO HERB SOUP

Ingredients

1 Tbs. olive oil

3/4 cup hacked onion

2 cloves garlic, hacked

1 Tbs. hacked new oregano or basil

1 tsp. hacked new thyme or 1/4 tsp. dried

5 cups diced new tomatoes (2 lb.)

1/2 cups low-sodium vegetable soup

2 1/2 Tbs. tomato glue

2 tsp. sugar

Arrangement

In huge pot, heat oil over medium warmth. Include onion, garlic, oregano or basil and thyme and cook, mixing often, until onion starts to soften, around 5 minutes. Include tomatoes and cook, blending infrequently, 5 minutes. Mix in stock, tomato glue and sugar. Season to taste with salt and newly ground pepper.

Heat soup to the point of boiling. Lessen heat; stew, revealed, 15 minutes. Utilizing submersion blender, process until smooth.

Spoon into serving bowls and enhancement with crisp herbs.

POTATO BEAN STEW

Ingredients

For the garlic plunge

6 garlic cloves, stripped

250ml/9fl oz additional virgin olive oil

1 tsp salt

1 tsp sherry vinegar

For the potato and bean stew

2 tbsp olive oil

50g/2oz breadcrumbs

3 red onions, stripped and finely cleaved

4 garlic cloves, cleaved

750g/1lb 10oz potatoes, unpeeled, cut into huge 3D shapes

250ml/9fl oz vegetable stock

4 tomatoes, stripped, cleaved

1 can cannellini beans, depleted

1 bunch new mint leaves

1 tbsp new parsley, cleaved

75g/2½oz spread

½ lemon, squeeze as it were

Step by step instructions to recordings

Technique

Preheat the broiler to 180C/350F/gas 4.

For the garlic plunge, place the garlic into a heating dish and sprinkle over the olive oil. Hurl well to cover, then dish in the broiler for 25 minutes, or until the garlic is delicate and brilliant.

Move the garlic and oil into a food processor, include the salt and sherry vinegar and mix to a smooth purée. Put in a safe spot.

For the potato and bean stew, heat the olive oil in a dish and tenderly fry the breadcrumbs for 3-4 minutes, or until softened. Include the onions and garlic and cook for 8-10 minutes, or until the onions are delicate and translucent.

Add the potatoes and stock to the dish, then decrease the warmth and permit to stew for 10-12 minutes.

Include the tomatoes and beans and stew for another 4-5 minutes, then mix in the herbs, spread and lemon juice.

To serve, spoon the stew into serving bowls. Serve the garlic plunge close by, or spoon over the stew.

CHICKEN MUSHROOM SOUP

Ingredients

2 tablespoons margarine

1 tablespoon olive oil

1 pound boneless chicken bosoms, diced

1/2 cup diced carrot

1 enormous rib celery, diced

12 to 16 ounces cut mushrooms, a blend of new mushroom assortments, if wanted

1 clove garlic, minced

4 green onions, cut

2 tablespoons flour

4 cups chicken juices

1/2 teaspoon dried leaf thyme

1/2 teaspoon salt, or to taste

Crisp ground dark pepper

3/4 cup substantial cream

Technique

In an enormous pot, heat spread and olive oil over medium-low warmth. Include the onion and garlic and mix until delicate however not seared.

Include diced chicken, carrot, and celery; cook, blending, until chicken is about cooked through.

Include the mushrooms and keep cooking, blending, until mushrooms are delicate. Mix in flour until mixed; include chicken soup and thyme.

Bring to a stew, blending. Spread and decrease warmth to low; cook for around 10 to 16 minutes, until vegetables are delicate. Add salt and pepper to taste; mix in cream and warmth through.

TURKEY GREEN BEAN SOUP

Ingredients

2 cloves garlic, squashed and finely cleaved

2 tablespoons olive oil

1 onion, slashed

1 carrot, finely slashed

1 stalk celery, finely slashed

1 tablespoon slashed crisp sage leaves, if wanted

2 containers (32 oz each) Progresso™ chicken juices

1 narrows leaf

2 cups green beans, cut into 1-inch pieces*

1 sweet potato, diced*

1/2 cup uncooked little pasta, for example, orzo or pastina

3 cups diced cooked dim turkey meat

Steps

In an enormous soup pot, heat garlic in the olive oil. Permit to dark colored somewhat and include onion, carrot and celery. Spread; sweat over medium-low heat until softened, 7 or 8 minutes. Add the hacked sage to the soup pot alongside the juices and the sound leaf. Bring to a stew. When stewing, include the green beans, sweet potato and pasta to the soup. Bring it back up to a stew; lower warmth and cook for around 10 minutes or until vegetables are delicate and pasta is cooked. Mix in turkey. Turn the warmth off. Spread, and permit to sit and steam for 5 to 7 minutes.

Master Tips

3 cups remaining cooked Thanksgiving side vegetables can be utilized instead of the new vegetables.

GINGER CARROT SOUP

Ingredients

2 tablespoons sweet cream margarine

2 onions, stripped and slashed

6 cups chicken juices

2 pounds carrots, stripped and cut

2 tablespoons ground crisp ginger

1 cup whipping cream

Salt and white pepper

Harsh cream

Parsley sprigs, for decorate

Bearings

In a 6-quart dish, over medium high warmth, include margarine and onions and cook, mixing often, until onions are limp. Include juices, carrots, and ginger. Spread and heat to the point of boiling. Decrease warmth and stew until carrots are delicate when punctured.

Expel from warmth and move to a blender. Try not to fill the blender the greater part way, do it in clumps if you need to. Spread the blender and afterward hold a kitchen towel over the highest point of the blender*. Be cautious when mixing hot fluids as the blend can spurt out of the blender. Heartbeat the blender to begin it and afterward puree until smooth. Come back to the container and include cream, mix over high warmth until hot. For a smoother flavor heat soup to the point of boiling, include salt and pepper, to taste.

Spoon into bowls and enhancement with spot acrid cream and parsley sprigs.

CHICKEN BRUSSELS SOUP

Much like its cruciferous cousin, cauliflower, Brussels sprouts transform into a superbly rich and velvety soup just by cooking this vegetable with aromatics and spinning it up in a stock. This beef winds up having an a lot further nutty flavor than you may expect, just as a thicker, more fulfilling surface than you would envision that these minor cabbages might contain.

You can include a touch of cream for a considerably creamier impact, however it isn't vital since this beef holds up individually without the additional cream.

This Brussels grows formula is a beautiful first course to an extravagant supper, in the interim, fills in as a delightful base for a vegan supper with a green serving of mixed greens and some generous entire grain bread for a total feast.

Ingredients

1 pound brussels grows

1 rib celery

1 huge shallot or little leek

1 to 2 tablespoons spread

1/2 teaspoon fine ocean salt, in addition to additional to taste

3 cups chicken stock or vegetable juices

Steps to Make It

Accumulate the ingredients.

Trim off and dispose of the stem parts of the bargains grows. Generally slash the sprouts, if they are enormous. The Brussels sprouts will get puréed at last, so while even pieces will cook all the more equally, this isn't a stunner challenge. Regardless of how you have prepared them saved them.

Trim and generally cleave the celery; strip and generally hack the shallot or leek.

Warmth the margarine in a little pot over medium-high warmth. When it is dissolved, include the celery and the shallot. Sprinkle with the salt and cook, mixing regularly, until the vegetables are delicate, around 3 minutes.

Include the cleaved Brussels sprouts and mix to consolidate. Cook, mixing every so often until the Brussels sprouts turn a more brilliant shade of green, around 2 minutes. Include the stock and heat everything just to the point of boiling.

Diminish the warmth to keep up an unfaltering stew, spread somewhat, and cook until the Brussels sprouts are totally delicate around 10 minutes.

Utilize a hand-held submersion blender to totally purée the soup. (You can likewise do this in a blender, however simply make certain to give the soup a chance to cool somewhat first, work in bunches, and put a kitchen towel over the highest point of the blender in the event that the warmth of the soup makes it splatter out.) Be certain to purée the soup somewhat longer than you may might suspect is important; you need the last item to be as smooth as could reasonably be expected.

Mix in cream, if you like.

Serve the soup hot, with an embellishment of crisply ground dark pepper to taste.

Use Caution When Blending Hot Ingredients

Steam grows rapidly in a blender, and can make ingredients splatter all over or cause consumes. To anticipate this, fill the blender only 33% of the route up, vent the top, and spread with a collapsed kitchen towel while mixing.

CHAPTER 4: FREESTYLE CHICKED AND POULTRY

MEXICAN BEAN CHICKEN

Ingredients

1 tbsp olive oil

1 onion , cut

2 red peppers, deseeded and hacked into largish pieces

3 tbsp chipotle glue

2 x 400g jars hacked tomatoes

4 skinless chicken bosoms

140g quinoa

2 chicken stock 3D squares

1 x 400g can pinto beans, depleted little pack coriander, most cleaved, a couple of leaves left entirety juice 1 lime

1 tbsp sugar normal yogurt, to serve

Technique

Warmth the oil in a profound griddle and fry the onions and peppers for a couple of mins until softened. Mix in the chipotle glue for a moment, trailed by the tomatoes. Mean a tomato can-brimming with water to cover the chicken and bring to a delicate stew. Include the chicken bosoms and tenderly stew, turning the chicken every so often, for 20 mins until the chicken is cooked through.

Carry a huge pan of water to the overflow with the stock solid shapes. Include the quinoa and cook for 15 mins until delicate, including the beans for the last min. Channel well and mix in the coriander and lime juice, then check for flavoring before covering to keep warm.

Lift the chicken out onto a board and shred each bosom utilizing two forks. Mix again into the tomato sauce with the sugar and season. Present with the quinoa, dispersing the stew with some coriander leaves just before dishing up and eating with a bit of yogurt as an afterthought.

CHEESE CREAM CHICKEN

I simply need to take a fast moment to express an exceptionally cheerful birthday to my now 6-year-old child, whose birthday is today.

He's my infant who's not under any condition a child nowadays. In any case, he's as yet my sweet, glad, excessively savvy, attractive blonde kid that I could simply gobble straight up.

So you know I'm about the simple chicken suppers right?

Well this is an overly basic, scrumptiously velvety chicken formula I've been making for two or three years now and simply needed to impart to you!

Simple cream cheddar chicken has delicate portions of chicken that are cooked and covered in a yummy cream cheddar blend, alongside certain onions and mushrooms.

Everything gets sprinkled with mozzarella cheddar, which melts down over the chicken and veggies toward the end.

It's so delightful and it's ideal for class kickoff season when I need something that is speedy however encouraging. Something simple yet that the entire family will cheerfully plunk down to around evening time.

(Furthermore, despite the fact that this is extremely simple and essential, I've even made it for organization. My relative said I should give her the formula!)

This formula is prepared in around 25 minutes, which I love, regardless of what night of the week it is.

(We generally talk about occupied weeknights, yet my ends of the week aren't a period I especially need to slave away in the kitchen on an included supper either. Any other individual?)

What's more, I love this has no overwhelming cream, which I never appear to have.

Truth be told, it's just got 7 primary ingredients! 🙌

That sumptuously smooth sauce that covers the chicken and mushrooms is simply cream cheddar and some chicken stock. It melts down with every one of the flavors from the sautéed onions and mushrooms and the singed bits from the chicken and makes such a tasty sauce.

(I've utilized that stunt before with chicken bosom with jalapeño cheddar sauce and sound rich Italian chicken skillet, among others.)

What's more, because of that sauce, you're unquestionably going to need to serve this over some feathery steamed rice.

If you know me, you realize I go for the entire grains. However, it can take 30-35 minutes to make darker rice.

Not actually perfect if everything else can be prepared well before that.

So today I needed to impart to you another market discover: VeeTee rice.

It cooks in the microwave, in its own compartment, in only 2 minutes. That is correct, 2 minutes.

It gets impeccably feathery and hot and prepared to serve.

We generally use it at dinnertime, however it would be extraordinary for lunch grain bowls as well.

I love their wholegrain dark colored rice the best for ordinary, however they have huge amounts of other delectable assortments as well: standard long grain rice, basmati rice, wholegrain darker rice and quinoa, and the sky is the limit from there, including some fun seasoned rice choices.

You can discover VeeTee on the web yet in addition at Harris Teeter (my neighborhood store) and Walmart Grocery. See what flavors you can bring home because this is a genuine help!

My other most loved efficient stunt: shop your plans on the web.

I've become acquainted with the people over at Myxx and I'm enamored with their story and their administration.

HERE'S THE QUICK RUN-DOWN ON MYXX:

Myxx was begun by two occupied mothers who needed a simpler method to bolster their families sound, home cooked dinners. (See why I love them?)

Their administration enables plans to be shop-capable.

That implies when you go down to the formula card underneath, you can click their catch and add the ingredients you have to your truck.

What truck? Ok, that is the magnificence. You get the opportunity to pick which nearby market you shop at (they incorporate with huge amounts of stores).

They'll let you know if an item is out of stock, if something is at a bargain, and what sizes or assortments are accessible. (They incorporate with the store's stock so it's consistently state-of-the-art. Splendid.)

Also, you can decide to simply print your rundown (which is sorted out by your nearby store's format) to take to the store to do the shopping yourself. Or then again you can pick curbside get if your nearby store offers that element. Or on the other hand you can pick from conveyance choices, once more, contingent upon what your neighborhood chose store has accessible.

Alright, presently how about we return to this heavenly saucy chicken! 😋

I are very brave, tips and substitutions coming up beneath. Only tryin' to be useful.

(Also, you all realize I like to assist you with making this formula your own special!)

If you need to bounce on down to the formula, essentially look through the remainder of the content. The formula card is close to the base of the page, over the remarks segment.

NOTES ON EASY CREAM CHEESE CHICKEN:

You can utilize more than the 1/2 lbs. of chicken in this formula, yet you'll need to expand the cream cheddar and chicken stock to make additional sauce. The sauce is SOOO great!

I love the mushrooms in with this formula yet you could skip them if you don't have any close by – or don't care for them. I've made this without mushrooms previously and it was as yet tasty.

The formula requires the 1/3-less fat cream cheddar and it's delightfully smooth. Go for the genuine book if you like, yet I don't prescribe utilizing fat free cream cheddar.

If you don't have any chicken juices, you could substitute vegetable soup or simply use water.

I love the melty mozzarella on top however you could likewise attempt this presented with ground Parmesan if you like.

The parsley is great as a trimming yet includes a pleasant herby freshness as well. Don't hesitate to skip it or to utilize some dried herbs as a flavoring on the chicken if you'd like.

As may be, this formula is without gluten, low carb and keto-accommodating. 👍

Additionally, a speedy word about the chicken in this formula.

I cut my boneless, skinless chicken bosoms into long strips.

That guarantees all the more in any event, cooking and furthermore causes stretch the chicken to encourage more individuals. It likewise cooks all the more rapidly. Win, win, win!

It's one of my preferred stunts. (See my simple balsamic chicken and salsa chicken for other snappy and simple chicken plans that utilization this equivalent easy route.)

If you'd want to utilize full chicken bosoms that haven't been cut, simply increment the cooking time to represent the expanded thickness.

You could likewise dice up the chicken bosoms into 1-inch 3D squares if you'd preferably have littler pieces. Simply make certain to turn them more as they singe and don't overcook them.

Furthermore, since alternatives satisfy me, don't hesitate to utilize boneless, skinless chicken thighs for this formula as well. They'll simply require some extra cook time to get cooked entirely through.

CHICKEN VEGGIE RICE

Ingredients

for 4 servings

oil, of your inclination, to taste

1 lb boneless, skinless chicken bosom (455 g), cubed

salt, to taste

pepper, to taste

1 lime, squeezed

⅓ cup new cilantro (15 g), minced

1 red chime pepper, diced

½ red onion, diced

2 cloves garlic, minced

1 sack riced cauliflower

1 cup corn (175 g), steamed

½ teaspoon bean stew powder, discretionary

1 can dark beans, flushed and depleted, discretionary

lime, cut into wedges, discretionary

Readiness

Warmth favored cooking oil in a huge skillet over medium-high warmth. Include chicken, season with salt and pepper, and cook until cooked through and never again pink.

Include lime juice and cilantro. Mix to join. Expel chicken from skillet, place on a plate, and put in a safe spot.

Add somewhat more oil to skillet if required, then include red onion, ringer pepper, and garlic. Mix to join. Permit to cook until onion starts to turn straightforward, blending every so often.

Include riced cauliflower, corn, and bean stew powder. Cook until cauliflower is delicate and expel from heat.

Appropriate dark beans, chicken, and cauliflower blend equitably between 4 holders. Top with a wedge of lime.

This dinner prep can be refrigerated for as long as 4 days.

Appreciate!

TURKEY APPLE PATTIES

There's a superior breakfast meat around the local area. What's more, it's made with no additional fillers, additives, sugar or garbage. What's more, it's child well-disposed and mother affirmed. What's more, tried and true (read: I've made these Turkey Apple Sausage Patties for my family a bigger number of times than I can check since our genuine food adventure began over seven years prior).

This formula came to fruition for 3 reasons:

I was disappointed that each morning meal frankfurter available contained ingredients I was attempting to expel from our eating regimen.

I required a financial limit amicable protein option in contrast to eggs and I could purchase natural ground turkey at Costco for under $4.00/lb.

My children think everything is "excessively hot" – particularly breakfast wiener. Be that as it may, these aren't zesty except if you need them to be.

Extra focuses for the way that these Turkey Apple Sausage Patties are additionally cooler neighborly which makes them a simple option to Crispy Grain-Free Waffles, Paleo Vegan Pancakes, a 5-Ingredient Go-To Green Smoothie or even my hubby's adored eggs over medium with sauteed greens and hand crafted sauerkraut.

Continuously read the ingredients!

Have you at any point investigated the ingredients in locally acquired breakfast meats, for example, hotdog patties? If not, how about we investigate a portion of the ingredients you may discover in a prevalent locally acquired brand. Ingredients incorporate pork, water, potassium lactate, salt, zest, sugar, sodium phosphates, dextrose, monosodium glutamate, sodium diacetate, and caramel shading. When extremely, the name SHOULD peruse: pork, flavors, salt. Right?!

This is a decent suggestion to consistently skirt the mark asserts on the facade of the bundle and go directly to the ingredients on bundled food things. If you can't articulate an ingredient or it looks as though it has a place in a science class, it's ideal to remain on the rack where it has a place. Even better, stick to custom made foods like these Turkey Apple Sausage Patties, made with only a bunch of ingredients you most likely as of now have close by.

Twofold the formula and feed the cooler with these Turkey Apple Sausage Patties.

I'm tied in with having prepared arranged foods close by for when I need them and these Turkey Apple Sausage Patties are ideal for solidifying. I generally cause a twofold group of this formula with the goal that I to have bounty to solidify for future dinners. Because you know, if you feed the cooler you feed yourself one more day. Furthermore, with very. little. exertion.

Season as you wish...

I understand that you don't generally have everything close by for a formula and that occasionally the exact opposite thing you need to do is headed out to the store for a touch of either zest. Which is the reason I've attempted these Turkey Apple Sausage Patties with a bunch of zest mixes and different apples (read: whatever I had close by) and they generally end up incredible. The key is to have, at the absolute minimum, salt and garlic powder. The remainder of the flavors can be switched up contingent upon what you like and what you have close by.

Try not to like fennel? Forget about it. Need a without nightshade or AIP-accommodating alternative? Forget about the paprika. Try not to have dried sage? Substitute Italian flavoring or dried thyme. Need to utilize crisp sage or thyme? Twofold the sums recorded in the formula. Need it fiery? Take a stab at utilizing hot smoked paprika or a touch of ground white pepper or red pepper pieces. You truly can't turn out badly whichever way with these Turkey Apple Sausage Patties because you're getting a sound portion of protein and none of the garbage you don't need like nitrates, nitrites, sugar, artificial hues, MSG, and so forth.

INGREDIENTS

1 lb. ground dull meat turkey (may substitute ground chicken)

½ cup finely minced apples (any assortment will work)

½ tsp. garlic powder

½ tsp. Italian flavoring or dried sage

½ tsp. paprika

1/4 tsp. squashed fennel (discretionary; pulverize gently utilizing a mortar and pestle)

½ tsp. salt

¼ tsp. dark pepper

1–2 Tbsp. coconut oil or avocado oil

Directions

Consolidate turkey (or chicken), diced apple, flavors, salt, and pepper in a blending bowl. Blend altogether with an enormous spoon or your hands.

Utilizing wet hands, structure meat blend into 12 little patties (Thin is great because they will therapist and fill out in the dish a piece).

Warmth a huge skillet over medium-high warmth. When the skillet is hot, include oil/fat (about ½ Tbsp. per bunch of patties, contingent upon the size of your container).

Add the patties to the dish, being mindful so as not to stuff them or it's difficult to flip them and they won't dark colored also. Cook for around 4-5 minutes for every side until sautéed and never again pink in the middle.

Expel patties to a plate fixed with a paper towel and rehash with residual oil and turkey blend.

Store in a canvassed holder in the icebox for as long as 4 days – might be solidified for longer stockpiling.

MARINARA CHEESE CHICKEN

When needing a Chicken Parmigiana and no opportunity to make it, I decide on this brisk rendition, covered in tomato sauce and beat with softened mozzarella cheddar. If you don't have the opportunity to make a café quality supper yet you're desiring those flavors, this formula is for you! Mozzarella Chicken In Tomato Sauce consistently wins!

The chicken bosoms are scoured with seasonings and seared until brilliant and cooked through. Then, I include some minced garlic, pour our preferred marinara sauce in to the skillet, season with basil and any seasonings you love, top them with cheddar, sear (or flame broil) them in the broiler for 2-3 minutes, and supper is on the table in under 15 minutes.

Present with a serving of mixed greens, or extra rice or pasta, or steamed vegetables. The decision is yours (as usual)!

Preheat broiler to 350 degrees F (175 degrees C). Gently oil a rimmed heating sheet.

Spot beaten eggs in a shallow bowl. Spot bread morsels in a different bowl and blend in with 1/2 cup of the destroyed cheddar.

Dunk chicken bosoms in the egg blend. Coat chicken bosoms on all sides with bread pieces. Spot chicken bosoms on arranged preparing sheet.

Prepare in preheated stove 20 minutes. Expel sheet from stove and top each bosom with some marinara sauce. Sprinkle the rest of the cheddar over the bosoms.

Prepare until cheddar has liquefied and sauce is bubbly, around 10 additional minutes. A moment read thermometer embedded into the inside should peruse at any rate 165 degrees F (74 degrees C).

TURKEY BEAN CHILI

Make this low-calorie bean stew in only 20 minutes for a snappy, one-pot dinner. Present with cornbread to finish the feast.

Ingredients

1 cup prechopped red onion

1/3 cup hacked seeded poblano pepper (around 1)

1 teaspoon packaged minced garlic

1/4 pounds ground turkey

1 tablespoon stew powder

2 tablespoons tomato glue

2 teaspoons dried oregano

1 teaspoon ground cumin

1/4 teaspoon salt

1/4 teaspoon dark pepper

1 (19-ounce) can cannellini beans, washed and depleted

1 (14.5-ounce) can diced tomatoes, undrained

1 (14-ounce) can without fat, lower-sodium chicken stock

1/2 cup hacked crisp cilantro

6 lime wedges

Step by step instructions to Make It

Warmth an enormous pan over medium warmth. Include initial 4 ingredients; cook for 6 minutes or until turkey is done, mixing every now and again to disintegrate. Mix in bean stew powder and next 8 ingredients (through soup); heat to the point of boiling. Diminish warmth, and stew 10 minutes. Mix in cilantro. Present with lime wedges.

Culinary expert's Notes

Tip: To spare time, hack off the highest point of a washed cilantro bundle as opposed to picking individual leaves. The flimsy stems toward the top are delicate.

ORANGE PINEAPPLE CHICKEN

Sweet, tart and succulent with a contact of kick, this Pineapple Orange BBQ Chicken takes under 10 minutes of planning time and the moderate cooker wraps up.

This dish includes a fun interchange of flavors that go after consideration sufficiently long to be seen and afterward mix together in solidarity as they hypnotize your sense of taste.

This moderate cooker dish additionally makes a lot of sauce so it loans itself splendidly to presenting with rice or pureed potatoes. Simply include a veggie and you're good to go.

Ingredients (12)

1 can (20 oz.) DOLE® Pineapple Chunks, depleted, juice saved

2 cups MINUTE® Brown Rice, uncooked

1/2 tsp. red chilies, squashed, discretionary

1/4 cup cashews, toasted and cleaved

1 lb. chicken bosoms, cut into 1/2-inch pieces

2 tbsp. universally handy flour

1 tbsp. vegetable oil

1 cup red ringer pepper, slashed

1 cup sugar snap peas

2/3 cup KIKKOMAN® Sweet and Sour Sauce

1/4 cup KIKKOMAN Less Sodium Soy Sauce

1 orange(s), zested and squeezed

Headings

Measure held pineapple squeeze and add enough water to make 1-3/4 cups fluid. Get ready rice as indicated by bundle headings utilizing juice-water blend. Coat chicken pieces with flour.

Warmth oil in enormous skillet or wok over medium-high warmth and cook chicken until edges are brilliant darker, around 5 to 7 minutes. Include pineapple, chime pepper and snap peas. Cook until marginally softened, around 3 minutes.

Include prepared sauce, soy sauce, squeezed orange and red chilies to dish. Mix and cook an extra 3 minutes or until sauce starts to bubble. Mix in orange get-up-and-go. Serve over rice bested with cashews and green onions.

BBQ TURKEY MEATBALLS

This is another of my endeavors at helping up comfort food. I don't have a clue how in reality light they are, yet they're made with ground turkey, are without oil, have just a tiny piece of salt, are prepared, and could absolutely deal with something green and healthified added to the blend... something like cooked spinach possibly? I would have gone there if I'd had any helpful, however I didn't, and you know how I feel about setting off to the supermarket.

Anyway. These are fundamentally similar to turkey meatloaf amped up with additional flavoring and BBQ sauce and afterward folded into minimal two-nibble meatballs.

They get carmelized in a skillet actually rapidly and afterward sprinkled with somewhat more BBQ sauce, and afterward heated.

These would most likely be enjoyed particularly on toothpicks as hors d'oeuvres at a gathering. It's football season, isn't that so? These future preferred a great deal for that.

We had them for supper with a major green serving of mixed greens, broiled Brussels sprouts, and cauliflower crush

Ingredients

1-1.5 pounds ground turkey

½ cup onion, finely minced

1 egg

¼ cup breadcrumbs

1 teaspoon garlic powder

1 teaspoon stew powder

½ teaspoon paprika

½ teaspoon legitimate salt

¾ cup BBQ sauce, separated

2 tablespoons oil

Directions

Pre-heat the stove to 375. Line a preparing sheet with material paper (not completely required yet makes for a lot simpler cleanup!).

In a huge bowl, utilizing your hands, combine every one of the ingredients with the exception of the BBQ sauce and oil.

Blend in 3-4 tablespoons of the BBQ sauce; enough to assist it with authoritative and include enhance. If you sense that your blend is too damp include more breadcrumbs.

Warmth the oil in the skillet.

Fold the turkey blend into 1½ inch balls and drop into the warmed skillet in clusters (I cook around 8 at once) Roll them around following a moment so they dark colored generally uniformly. Evacuate the cooked meatballs to the readied heating sheet and rehash until they are altogether carmelized.

Spoon the remaining BBQ sauce over every meatball and prepare for 15-20 minutes, until they are cooked through.

Present with more BBQ sauce if you're feeling saucy.

Notes

I typically get around 36 meatballs from this formula.

CHICKEN MUSHROOM MEATBALLS

These chicken meatballs are delicious and light not at all like some other chicken meatballs that can be odd and hard. What's more, can fly around when you have a go at cutting into them. Like evading you. Didn't transpire 🙈

There are some cool tips to making this formula, quicker, less complex simpler which I'm going to share.

cooking tips for rich chicken meatballs in mushroom sauce

While making meatballs, the most ideal route is to blend every one of your ingredients with the exception of the ground meat first. Along these lines it's a lot simpler to join your flavoring, restricting specialists and enhancing when you at last include the meat.

Don't over blend. Truly, simply stop when you have a feeling that you are 90% done. Workaholic behavior the meat can prompt denser meatballs.

To hack the mushrooms finely, simply cut them down the middle and add them to a food processor. This will coarsely cleave the mushrooms without you doing any of that exertion. Takes about 2.5 minutes.

Continuously burn the meatballs on high warmth. This secures in the flavors and the singe causes them hold their shape when you add them back to the sauce.

Don't hesitate to switch up chicken meatballs for vegan ones if you are a veggie lover. Be that as it may, hold the sauce. Because that sauce totally shakes!

Succulent chicken meatballs are critical to this formula and here are a few hints that you can utilize everytime you make meatballs to keep them delicate and delicious:

Blend the include ins first: While blending meatballs, I have a stage that I never miss. I include all the include ins like breadcrumbs, egg, flavoring and so on to the bowl and combine them first so when I include my ground meat, it's a lot simpler to join the flavors and there is no way of over blending

Don't overmix: To shield meatballs from getting extreme while cooking, don't overmix the blend. Try not to utilize power while blending, and simply hurl everything together and unquestionably utilize your hands which will give you better control. If your blend looks pale, you've gone excessively far

Try not to overcook: It's anything but difficult to overcook chicken meat. For this situation, I burn the meatballs in the skillet to secure the flavors and afterward stew the meatballs in the sauce till they are cooked through. These meatballs need 15-20 minutes of cooking time.

These velvety chicken meatballs in mushroom sauce are delicate, delicious, brimming with season and hurled in a delectable sauce made up with bunches of mushrooms. This is a delightful brief dish that is ideal for supper with certain noodles or pasta.

INGREDIENTS

For the Meatballs:

¾ cup Bread Crumbs

1 Egg

1 teaspoon Oregano

1 teaspoon Paprika

3 Garlic Cloves, minced

¼ cup ground Parmesan

550 grams/1.25 pounds ground Chicken

Salt to taste

2 tablespoons Olive Oil

For the Sauce:

2 tablespoon Olive Oil

1 tablespoon Butter

2 Garlic Cloves, minced

½ cup slashed Onions

1 cup finely slashed Mushrooms

2 tablespoons Flour

1 ½ cups low sodium Chicken Broth

1 teaspoon dried Rosemary

1/2 teaspoon dried Parsley

½ teaspoon Paprika

Salt and Pepper to taste

½ cup Heavy Cream

Guidelines

Make the meatballs: In an enormous bowl, combine every one of the ingredients aside from ground chicken and oil. Blend well and include the ground chicken. Blend till simply joined. Structure the blend into roughly 18 meatballs. Put in a safe spot.

Singe: Heat two tablespoons Olive Oil in a skillet and include the same number of meatballs as will fit into the container without congestion. You may need to do this in clumps. On high warmth, darker the meatballs on all sides and evacuate them on a plate.

Sauce: Heat two tablespoons olive oil and a tablespoon of spread in a similar dish. Include garlic and onions. Cook till the onions soften and become translucent. Include the mushrooms and cook for another 2-3 minutes. Mix in the flour and cook for one more moment to dispose of the crude flour enhance. Gradually include the chicken juices and continue whisking persistently till the sauce thickens. Mix in the rosemary, parsley, paprika, salt, pepper and meatballs. Include somewhat more stock or water if the sauce is excessively thick. Stew the meatballs for ten minutes. Mix in the substantial cream and switch off the fire. Serve hot with noodles, rice or pureed potatoes.

NOTES

To hack the mushrooms finely, simply cut them down the middle and add them to a food processor. This will coarsely cleave the mushrooms without you doing any of that exertion. Takes about 2.5 minutes.

TURKEY VEGETABLE MIX

Do you ever have those evenings where you return home from work or have quite recently had a bustling day and truly don't want to cook. Well as hard as it might be to accept, food bloggers have those days as well. Sure we love food and are always in the kitchen making new plans to impart to the world, yet some of the time it's those days that we least want to make supper for our very own families. This is the place the Turkey and Vegetable Skillet proves to be useful.

Have I at any point revealed to you that over food blogging I additionally cook suppers week after week for a lady and her significant other? I began doing this about a year back when we moved to Colorado and have delighted in each moment of it. Over the previous year I have gone from cooking meat dishes, to veggie lover, and now I even cook vegetarian suppers for them. Preparing veggie lover suppers has really enabled me to try different things with a variety of dairy and meat options that I probably won't have regularly attempted. Having the option to try different things with different foods and cooking systems keeps the activity fun and energizing.

This anyway takes me back to occupied days and not wanting to prepare supper. The inclination when you don't want to cook is to either go out or pop something in the microwave. Both of these alternatives are obviously quick and advantageous, yet not really the most solid of decisions. That is the reason on days when I've gone through a large portion of the day remaining in the kitchen cooking and the other half drifting over the table taking pictures of food I need something that I can put together effectively and that I won't need to do a lot of tidy up for a while later. This Turkey and Vegetable Skillet possesses all the necessary qualities for both of these situations.

To make this generous and scrumptious skillet supper I essentially seared some ground turkey in my cast iron skillet (a nonstick skillet fills in too), cleaved up a few of my preferred vegetables and added them to the turkey, then beat everything with some destroyed cheddar. Presently don't disclose to me you don't have 20 minutes to toss this dinner together. I decided to utilize zucchini, summer squash, green beans, and tomatoes as the vegetables in this skillet supper, however you could blend it up and utilize whatever you have close by. The destroyed cheddar over everything was most likely my preferred part. I utilized smoked mozzarella. Have you at any point had this stuff? Life changer, try it out! If you can't discover smoked mozzarella, standard mozzarella, smoked gouda, or ordinary gouda would all work incredible. After you top the vegetables and turkey with the destroyed cheddar, put it in the broiler set on cook. Doing this melts the cheddar, yet makes a decent mushy covering. I could conceivably have torn portion of the smoky, gooey outside off the top and made that my supper. No second thoughts, it tasted great! Whenever you get back home from a bustling day, mull over halting through that drive-through or getting a microwave supper out of the cooler. Rather, take a stab at making this new and simple to make Turkey and Vegetable Skillet!

INGREDIENTS

2 t. olive oil

1/2 pound lean ground turkey

1/2 cup onion, diced

2 cloves of garlic, minced

1 cup zucchini or summer squash, diced

1 cup new green beans, end cut

1 cup cherry tomatoes, split

1/2 cup fire cooked tomatoes

1 t. fit salt

1/2 t. dried basil

1/2 t. dried oregano

1/4 t. dark pepper

1/2 cup smoked mozzarella, destroyed (standard mozzarella, gouda, or smoked gouda may likewise be utilized)

Guidelines

Preheat broiler to cook.

In an enormous broiler evidence skillet over medium high warmth, heat the olive oil.

When the oil is hot include the ground turkey and split it up until it's in little pieces.

When the turkey is nearly cooked through include the onion and garlic.

Cook for 1 moment and afterward include the remainder of the vegetables.

Cook for another 4-5 minutes or until the vegetables have softened somewhat.

Top the turkey and vegetable blend with the destroyed cheddar.

Put the skillet in the stove and cook it just until the cheddar is liquefied and brilliant dark colored.

CHAPTER 5: FREESTYLE RED MEAT

ZUCCHINI CHILI BEEF

Ingredients

2 tablespoons extra-virgin olive oil

12 ounces ground hamburger throw

1 onion, cleaved

1 poblano chile pepper, seeded and cleaved

3 cloves garlic, minced

2 tablespoons bean stew powder

1 teaspoon ground cumin Kosher salt and crisply ground pepper

1 15-ounce can diced tomatoes with green chiles

1 15-ounce can pinto beans (don't deplete)

2 medium zucchini as well as yellow squash, cut into ½-inch pieces

1 avocado, diced

New cilantro, for garnish

Bearings

Warmth the olive oil in a huge pot or Dutch stove over medium-high warmth. Include the ground hamburger and cook, separating the meat, until seared, around 3 minutes. Include the onion, poblano and garlic; cook, blending every so often, until the vegetables are delicate and softly seared, around 5 minutes. Mix in the stew powder, cumin, 1 teaspoon salt and a couple of drudgeries of pepper. Cook, mixing, until consolidated, around 1 moment.

Include the tomatoes and the beans and their fluid to the pot; heat to the point of boiling, then lessen the warmth to medium and stew until the fluid is somewhat decreased, around 5 minutes.

Mix the squash into the pot. Incompletely spread and cook, mixing infrequently, until the squash is delicate and the bean stew thickens somewhat, around 10 minutes (signify ½ cup water if the stew is excessively thick). Season with salt. Top each serving of stew with the avocado and some cilantro.

BEEF LETTUCE BURGERS

Ingredients

Sauce:

1/4 cup Greek yogurt

2 tablespoons adobo sauce (from canned chipotles in adobo)

1 tablespoon Dijon mustard

2 runs Worcestershire sauce

Burgers:

2 pounds ground hurl

1 teaspoon genuine salt

1/2 teaspoon crisply ground dark pepper

5 runs Worcestershire sauce

Ingredients:

1 head ice sheet, green leaf or margarine lettuce

2 avocados, cut

1 tomato, cut

1/4 red onion, daintily cut into rings

12 little sweet pickles, cleaved

Bearings

For the sauce: Mix together the yogurt, adobo sauce, mustard and Worcestershire sauce in a little bowl. Put in a safe spot.

For the burgers: In a bowl, consolidate the ground toss, salt, dark pepper and Worcestershire sauce. Structure four patties and put in a safe spot.

Warmth a skillet over medium-high warmth. Cook the patties until done in the center, 4 to 6 minutes for each side.

For the Ingredients: Cut the base of every lettuce leaf on the head and cautiously strip it away so it remains as flawless as could be expected under the circumstances.

Top the patties with avocado cuts, tomato cuts, red onion rings and slashed pickles, then shower with the sauce to taste. Utilize a few lettuce leaves for each patty and fold them over the patty as firmly as possible. Cut into equal parts and serve right away!

CREAMUY PORK CHOPS

This is a one container supper which makes tidy up so a lot simpler. The seared pork slashes in a velvety garlic mushroom sauce are going to leave you so fulfilled! Café quality supper from the solace of your home at a small amount of the price. Indeed, it would be ideal if you

Did you realize that pork is the most regularly expended meat on the planet? It's a moderate decision of meat paying little respect to where you live, and, if cooked appropriately, it is delicious and tasty. It's no big surprise our broiled pork tenderloin is among the main 10 plans a seemingly endless amount of time after year.

The most effective method to Cook Pork Chops:

Season and singe pork slashes on a hot skillet in oil and margarine

Saute and season cut mushrooms

Include remaining ingredients for the rich mushroom sauce

Return pork cleaves, cover in sauce and cook until delicate

NOTE: The meat can't thicker than 1/2″ in thickness or else it won't cook through. If the meat is thicker, beat with a meat hammer until around 1/2″ in thickness.

The most effective method to Substitute for Bone-in Pork Chops:

This formula will work for both bone-in or boneless pork cleaves. If substituting for bone-in, cook an extra 2-3 minutes longer for every side, contingent upon the thickness of the meat. The inward perusing of the thickest piece of the pork slash should peruse 145°F which is the protected pork cooking temperature.

What Kind of Mushrooms Should I use?

Utilize whatever mushrooms you have close by. White mushrooms, cremini or portobello mushrooms will all work in this formula.

NOTE: Did you realize that portobello mushrooms are simply cremini mushrooms that are gathered when developed and completely developed?

Would i be able to Substitute the Hot Sauce?

The hot sauce gives the rich mushroom sauce a light kick. If you are worried about it being excessively zesty, include less of the sauce or overlook it totally, however it adds extraordinary flavor to the sauce.

How to Make the Pork Chops Tender?

When the pork hacks are added back to the container, turn the warmth down to low and permit the pork cleaves to keep cooking another 5-8. Be certain the warmth is truly low so it doesn't consume the sauce.

BEEF BROCOLI DINNER

Indeed, you read that accurately ... 20 minutes! As in, you are not exactly a large portion of a scene of Fixer Upper away from diving your chopsticks into a huge bowl of the most delightful, delicate, saucy Easy Beef and Broccoli.

The exemplary takeout dishes (think Orange Chicken, Pad Thai and Chicken Egg Rolls) were one of my numerous desires during my subsequent pregnancy. But instead than feel the oily blame often connected with the intensely salted and oil-doused eatery variants of those dishes, I chose a quick and crisp rendition of hamburger and broccoli was an unquestionable requirement!

It must be thick enough to cover the delicate cuts of meat and the broccoli florets, without burdening the whole dish. What's more, in particular, there must be simply enough sauce so the going with rice likewise gets an opportunity to absorb all that great garlicky sauce. Need to see with your own eyes? Tune in beneath!

INGREDIENTS

3 Tablespoons cornstarch, partitioned

1 pound flank steak, cut into slight 1-inch pieces

1/2 cup low sodium soy sauce

3 Tablespoons pressed light dark colored sugar

1 Tablespoon minced garlic

2 teaspoons ground crisp ginger

2 Tablespoons vegetable oil, partitioned

4 cups little broccoli florets

1/2 cup cut white onions

Guidelines

In an enormous bowl, whisk together 2 tablespoons cornstarch with 3 tablespoons water. Add the hamburger to the bowl and hurl to consolidate.

In a different little bowl, whisk together the staying 1 tablespoon cornstarch with the soy sauce, dark colored sugar, garlic and ginger. Put the sauce in a safe spot.

Warmth an enormous nonstick sauté container over medium warmth. Include 1 tablespoon of the vegetable oil and once it is hot, include the meat and cook, blending always until the hamburger is nearly cooked through. Utilizing an opened spoon, move the hamburger to a plate and put it in a safe spot.

Include the staying 1 tablespoon of vegetable oil to the container and once it is hot, include the broccoli florets and cut onions and cook, mixing at times, until the broccoli is delicate, around 4 minutes.

Return the hamburger to the dish then include the readied sauce. Heat the blend to the point of boiling and cook, mixing, for 1 moment or until the sauce thickens somewhat. Present with rice or noodles.

The sauce must reach boiling point all together for the cornstarch to fill in as a thickening operator.

ROAST TACE WRAPS

Ingredients

2 pounds hamburger shoulder

Fit salt

Naturally ground dark pepper

Extra-virgin olive oil

2 cloves garlic, crushed

1 enormous onion, cut

One 28-ounce can squashed tomatoes, (suggested: San Marzano)

1 tablespoon ancho chile powder

1 tablespoon cayenne pepper

1 tablespoon ground cumin

3 sound leaves

Vegetable oil, for profound searing

6 new medium corn tortillas

3 cups finely destroyed white cabbage

Guacamole, formula pursues

1/4 pack new cilantro leaves

Bearings

Season all sides of the meat with a considerable measure of salt and pepper. In an enormous Dutch broiler, or other substantial pot that has a tight spread, heat 2 tablespoons of olive oil over tolerably high warmth. Include the garlic and the hamburger to the pot, cooking the meat on all sides, setting aside the effort to get a pleasant covering outwardly. Add the onion and permit to daintily dark colored, around 3 to 4 minutes. Include the squashed tomatoes, in addition to 1 tomato container of water, flavors, season with salt and pepper, to taste, and add enough water to cover the meat. Heat to the point of boiling then diminish warmth and stew with a top for 3 hours until the meat is fork delicate. Give meat a chance to cool in the fluid. Shred meat and put in a safe spot.

Warmth a huge pot of oil over medium warmth. When oil arrives at 350 degrees F, fry the corn tortillas 1 at once. Spot the tortilla in the oil and hold up around 30 seconds. Then utilize the handle of a wooden spoon to press down into the focal point of the tortilla and crease it in the center. Hold down for a couple of moments trusting that the tortilla will shape into taco shell and afterward channel on paper towels. Season with salt.

To make salsa, beat every one of the ingredients, with the exception of the tomato juice, in a food processor. Include the held tomato juice if the salsa is excessively thick. Sprinkle salsa with olive oil, spread with saran wrap and put in a safe spot, enabling the flavors to wed.

To collect the tacos:

Lay some destroyed cabbage as a base. Top with some destroyed hamburger. Serve nearby Guacamole and salsa. Topping with crisp cilantro leaves.

Guacamole:

Split and pit the avocados. With a tablespoon, scoop out the substance into a blending bowl. Pound the avocados utilizing either a fork or potato masher, leaving them still somewhat thick. Include the rest of the ingredients, and crease everything together. Shower with a little olive oil, change flavoring with salt and pepper and give it 1 last blend in with a fork.

Lay a bit of cling wrap tight on the outside of the guacamole so it doesn't dark colored and refrigerate for at any rate 1 hour before serving.

GRILLED SPICED CHOPS
Cooking Method: Grilling

Dry rubs are additionally a terrific method to season pork hacks. Select hacks of near an inch in thickness — not much — then flame broil them over relentless medium warmth. We pick rib slashes over the inside cut assortment when cooking outside because their more noteworthy fat substance helps keep them damp, and we generally incline toward bone-in cleaves for their succulence. You may include a grill sauce the side with these, yet we relish their firm surface unvarnished

INGREDIENTS

Pork Chop Willy's Grilling Rub

3 tablespoons sweet paprika, ideally Spanish

1 tablespoon naturally ground dark pepper

1 tablespoon coarse salt, either fit or ocean salt

3/4 teaspoon sugar

3/4 teaspoon bean stew powder

3/4 teaspoon granulated garlic or garlic powder

3/4 teaspoon onion powder

1/4 to 1/2 teaspoon ground cayenne

Six to eight 10-to 11-ounce bone-in pork rib slashes, 3/4 to 1 inch thick

Vegetable oil shower

Planning

At any rate 1 and as long as 8 hours before you intend to flame broil the pork hacks, set up the dry rub, joining the ingredients in a little bowl. Coat the slashes with the zest blend, place them in a huge plastic sack, seal, and refrigerate.

Fire up the barbecue, carrying the warmth to medium (4 to 5 seconds with the hand test).

Expel the hacks from the icebox and let them sit secured at room temperature for around 20 minutes.

Shower the slashes with oil and move them to the flame broil. Flame broil for 18 to 20 minutes absolute. Turn onto each side twice, pivoting the cleaves a half turn each opportunity to get confound flame broil marks. The hacks are done when only a trace of pink stays at the inside. Serve hot.

CHAPTER 6: FREESTYLE FISH AND SEAFOOD

AVOCADO CRAB SALAD

This stuffed avocado and bump crab plate of mixed greens is light and new, made with lime juice, olive oil, cilantro and red onion. So snappy because there is no cooking included!

INGREDIENTS

1 medium Hass avocado, around 5 oz avocado

4 oz irregularity crab meat

2 tbsp cleaved red onion

1/2 tbsp crisp lime juice, from 1 lime

1 tbsp cleaved crisp cilantro

2 grape tomatoes, diced

1/2 tsp olive oil

1/4 tsp salt and new dark pepper

2 leaves spread lettuce, discretionary

Directions

In a medium bowl, consolidate onion, lime juice, cilantro, tomato, olive oil, 1/8 tsp salt and crisp pepper, to taste.

Include crab meat and delicately hurl.

Cut the avocado open, evacuate pit and strip the skin or spoon the avocado out.

Season with staying 1/8 tsp salt and fill the avocado parts similarly with crab serving of mixed greens.

This makes 2 servings, place on two plates with lettuce if you wish and serve.

POTATO MAYO FISH
INGREDIENTS

21 oz Wild Alaskan Pollock Filets

2 Pasture-Raised Eggs

2 Scallions

6 oz Green Beans

1¼ lbs Golden Potatoes

½ cup All-Purpose Flour

1¼ cups Panko Breadcrumbs

2 Tbsps Apple Cider Vinegar

¼ cup Mayonnaise

3 Tbsps Sweet White Miso Paste

1 Tbsp Vegetarian Ponzu Sauce

¼ cup Sweet Chili Sauce

2 Tbsps Crème Fraîche

1 Tbsp Togarashi Seasoning (Sweet Paprika, Hot Paprika, Dried Orange Peel, Poppy Seeds, White Sesame Seeds and Black Sesame Seeds)

Prep Bowls, 10 Piece Set

Keep in mind the significance of mise en place, French for "set up." Following a formula can prompt wreckage and turmoil in the kitchen—particularly if it's a formula you've never attempted. That is the reason the initial step of each Blue Apron formula is to prepare your ingredients so they are fit to be changed into something flavorful. This arrangement of 10 rich, chip-safe prep bowls will assist you with monitoring your kitchen while you cook and remain prepared at all times. Stackable and sturdy these dishwasher, cooler, and microwave safe bowls can deal with anything.

3 Tips To: Bread Like a Pro

In this video, including Austrian local Markus Glocker's chicken schnitzel (a mainstream yet off-menu thing at Bâtard in New York City), you'll figure out how to bread cutlets from probably the best gourmet specialist in the nation. There are three fundamental advances. The first is beating your cutlets to a ¼-inch thickness. For simple cleanup, place them on a work surface between two pieces of plastic. To pound the cutlets, Glocker utilizes an instrument called a meat tenderizer. In any case, it's anything but difficult to supplant at home with a level bottomed pot or skillet. Beating softens the meat by breaking separated its filaments, bringing about staggering surface. It additionally guarantees a fast, even cook and immaculate succulence. The subsequent advance is covering your cutlets in flour, to make a dry surface, then egg, to make a wet surface for the breadcrumbs to stick to. Be that as it may, be certain not to over-beat your egg: utilizing a fork (not a whisk), beat the egg just until the whites and yolks are fused. Joining them also completely will bring about a less vaporous soufflé (or puffy layer of cooked egg). At long last, in the wake of plunging the cutlets into the egg, coat them in the breadcrumbs.

Directions

1 Prepare the ingredients:

Fill a medium pot 3/4 of the path up with salted water; spread and warmth to bubbling on high. Wash and dry the crisp produce. Medium dice the potatoes. Cut the green beans into 1-inch pieces. Meagerly cut the scallions, isolating the white bottoms and empty greens tops.

2 Make the potato plate of mixed greens:

Add the diced potatoes to the pot of bubbling water and cook, revealed, 10 minutes. Include the green bean pieces. Keep on cooking 5 to 7 minutes, or until the vegetables are delicate when punctured with a fork. Mood killer the warmth. Channel completely and come back to the pot. Include the cut white bottoms of the scallions, vinegar, sweet bean stew sauce, crème fraîche, and 2 teaspoons of olive oil; season with salt and pepper. Mix to altogether consolidate.

3 Bread the fish:

While the potatoes cook, pat the fish dry with paper towels. Move to a cutting board; split each filet across. Season with salt and pepper on the two sides. Break the eggs into an enormous bowl. Include the miso glue; season with salt and pepper. Whisk overwhelmingly until smooth. Join the flour and a large portion of the togarashi on a huge plate; season with salt and pepper. Spot the breadcrumbs on a different huge plate; season with salt and pepper. Working two pieces one after another, altogether coat the prepared fish in the prepared flour (shaking off any overabundance), then in the beaten eggs (giving the abundance a chance to dribble off), then in the prepared breadcrumbs (squeezing to follow). Move to a different plate.

4 Cook the fish:

While the potatoes keep on cooking, in an enormous dish (nonstick, if you have one), heat a dainty layer of oil on medium-high. When the oil is hot enough that a spot of flour sizzles quickly when included, working in two groups, include the breaded fish. Cook 2 to 3 minutes for every side, or until carmelized and cooked through (including a slight layer of oil to the container between bunches). Move to a paper towel-fixed plate and promptly season with salt.

5 Make the ponzu mayo and serve your dish:

While the fish cooks, in a bowl, whisk together the mayonnaise and ponzu sauce. Season with salt and pepper. Serve the cooked fish and potato plate of mixed greens decorated with the cut green highest points of the scallions and remaining togarashi. Serve the ponzu mayo as an afterthought. Appreciate!

TUNA CRANBERRY SALAD

Fish, Cranberry, Pecan Salad Sandwich

The hubby was in radiant Las Vegas for a gathering and I was home not cooking our typical basics type supper. I can prepare sweets throughout the day, however it's often drudgery to think of supper thoughts.

Flame broiled cheddar, fried eggs and fish sandwiches are my go-to simple courses for when I'm going performance. Including dried cranberries for some sweetness and walnuts for crunch make for an overwhelming sandwich filling. What's more, a press of lemon juice added to the mayo is my unmistakable advantage, if you love fish serving of mixed greens, you should attempt this stacked Tuna, Cranberry, Pecan Salad Sandwich formula.

Tips for Making a Tuna Salad Sandwich

There's no explanation not to change this Tuna, Cranberry, Pecan Salad Sandwich formula to make it your own one of a kind.

Not an enthusiast of craisins? What about cut seedless grapes?

Nut hypersensitivity (or like my hubby "fake" nut sensitivity)? Forget about them, yet include a touch of additional celery for some crunch.

It is safe to say that you are a pickle fan? Diced sweet or dill would be terrific, and include some crisp dill if you like, as well.

Include a some stunning lettuce leaves and additionally cuts of crisp tomatoes to each sandwich.

Bill would lean toward his sandwich on cut white pastry shop bread rather than a decrepit roll, so select your preferred bread or rolls. I'm simply grateful he will eat fish. He asks for my fish dish each and every Lenten season. I'd preferably have this sandwich! If you're not a fish darling, this curried turkey plate of mixed greens sandwich is additionally awesome. Expectation you appreciate!!!

Ingredients

2 5 or 6 ounce jars great quality fish in oil or water, depleted

Juice of a large portion of a lemon

1/3 cup mayonnaise

1 shallot, minced

1/2-1 stalk of celery, diced

2 tablespoons dried cranberries

2 tablespoons cleaved walnuts

4 generous or dingy moves, cut

Lettuce, tomatoes, discretionary

Guidelines

Blend fish in with mayonnaise and lemon juice. Mix in shallots, celery, cranberries and walnuts. Tastes and add salt and pepper to taste.

Serve on moves with lettuce and tomatoes if wanted.

SALMON ASPARAGUS TREAT

Ingredients

4 sheets filo baked good

1 teaspoon diminished fat spread, softened

2 medium salmon filets (around 120g each)

10 asparagus lances

Naturally ground dark pepper

1 adjusted tablespoon low-fat delicate cheddar

Technique

1. Preheat the broiler to 190°C/Fan 170°C.

2. Line a heating plate with greaseproof paper.

3. Brush two of the filo baked good sheets with a tad bit of the softened decreased fat spread.

Then add another layer of baked good to each buttered sheet. Brush the second layers with the softened spread.

Spot the pieces of layered baked good one next to the other on the heating paper.

4. Spot a salmon filet in the focal point of each of the filo sheets, on the slanting.

Then place 5 asparagus sticks over every one of the filets.

Include some dark pepper and top with the low-fat delicate cheddar.

5. Overlap the sides of the cake over the filet to make a 'fold' around the salmon and press the closures together.

Brush with the remainder of the liquefied spread.

6. Prepare for 30 minutes, or until the baked good is fresh and brilliant.

7. Present with a lot of vegetables or a side plate of mixed greens.

Top tip

If you need to set up this before in the day, you can stop toward the finish of stage 4 and spot the heating plate in the ice chest until you're prepared to cook

BAKED SPICED FISH

Being a veggie lover, you would figure I will have an intense time cooking with meat and seafood. Yet, it's not. The explanation I am a veggie lover is because I have been raised one and I've been one for a really long time for me to build up a desire for meat and seafood and really like it. I simply treat them all as just ingredients and I don't discover them gross or inaccessible. Being hitched to a meat-a-holic helps as well, as I use him as a testing board for everything meat and seafood I make.

Chicken and meat has been simpler to make, as I probably am aware they can stand flavors, particularly in the Indian style arrangements and once I became accustomed to cooking with them and knew the ingredient, I wandered out to cooking with them in different foods and in the long run, building up my own plans with them. In any case, seafood was something I was constantly somewhat threatened by.

Fish and shell fish appeared to be excessively sensitive, that I was apprehensive I would over power them with flavors or more awful, overcook them. In any case, I couldn't deny my mallu-kid (the spouse is from Kerala, where seafood is devoured broadly and mallu is slang for the language Malayalam and furthermore somebody from Kerala) some great zesty seafood.

All Kerala seafood dishes are secured with flavors and coconut, that I knew if I attempted and tested a bit, I would in the long run hit the nail on the head. I utilized instant flavors for fish fry and make a snappy fish fry on the stove top for the spouse, now and again. I even wandered into making curries with prawns and I got that right. I was not open to making a decent fish curry, as of recently, where I concocted the ideal formula, for me in any event, so I cannot destroy it without tasting it Smile

This heated fish "fry" is a comparable formula, where you truly cannot turn out badly a lot. A decent zest marinade for the fish filets and pop it in the stove till the marinade is altogether cooked through. The fish turns out decent and enhanced. Proceed, attempt it, I realize you will adore it as much as my meat-a-holic did.

Ingredients

0.75 lb Mahi filet (2 filets of around 6-8 creeps long) or some other greasy fish

To pound together to a glue:

4 pearl onions

3 cloves garlic

1 inch ginger

1/2 tsp turmeric powder

1 tsp Kashmiri Chilie Powder

1 tsp dark pepper corns

1/2 tsp ocean salt

1 tsp coconut oil

1/2 lime squeezed

1/2 tsp garam masala

Guidelines

Put every one of the ingredients under "pound to frame a glue" in a mortar and pestle and crush to shape as fine a glue as could be allowed.

Cut the fish filets into two and make little cuts in them. Smear the glue similarly over every one of the filets and marinate in the cooler for 20-30 mins.

Pre heat stove to 375F

Line the fish on a heating plate with material paper on it and prepare for 20 mins. To polish it off, cook on high for 3-4 mins.

Present with crude red onion cuts and lime wedges.

Notes

To check for doneness: teh zest/masala glue on the fish ought to have changed shading marginally and not look excessively crude.

COD SHRIMP STEW

Ingredients

2 tablespoons olive oil

1 enormous onion, hacked

3 garlic cloves, minced

1 tablespoon minced crisp or 1 teaspoon dried thyme

1/4 teaspoon saffron strings or 1 teaspoon ground turmeric

2 narrows leaves

2 jars (14-1/2 ounces each) no-salt-included diced tomatoes

1 pound cod filet, cut into 1-inch solid shapes

1 pound uncooked enormous shrimp, stripped and deveined

2 cups water

1 can (14-1/2 ounces) vegetable juices

1 cup entire bit corn

1/4 teaspoon pepper

1 bundle (6 ounces) crisp child spinach

Lemon wedges, discretionary

Headings

In a 6-qt. stockpot, heat oil over medium warmth. Include onion; cook and mix until delicate. Include garlic, thyme, saffron and straight leaves. Cook and mix brief longer. Include tomatoes, fish, shrimp, water, stock, corn and pepper.

Heat to the point of boiling. Decrease heat; stew, revealed, 8-10 minutes or until shrimp turn pink and fish pieces effectively with a fork, including spinach during the last 2-3 minutes of cooking. Dispose of cove leaves. If wanted, present with lemon wedges.

Nourishment Facts

1-1/2 cups: 250 calories, 6g fat (1g soaked fat), 121mg cholesterol, 1005mg sodium, 18g starch (7g sugars, 3g fiber), 27g protein.

SHRIMP BLUE CHEESE SALAD

So natural to make, made with margarine lettuce, avocado, tomatoes and corn and completed with a sprinkle of olive oil.

Spring for me generally implies less solace food, and increasingly generous servings of mixed greens for lunch and supper. A portion of my go-to's are Rosemary Chicken Salad with Avocado and Bacon, Carne Asada Steak Salad, or Crock Pot Chicken and Black Bean Taco Salad, just to give some examples yet I simply love a plate of mixed greens with shrimp and avocado (Zesty Lime Shrimp and Avocado Salad is a top choice)!

I as of late got my hands on my companion Jessica's new cookbook The Pretty Dish: More than 150 Everyday Recipes and 50 Beauty DIYs to Nourish Your Body Inside and Out (affil interface) and realized I needed to make this! Her cookbook is beautiful, and loaded up with plans, alongside themed menus, party thoughts, executioner playlists, and DIY excellence ventures. Such a fun and beautiful cookbook!

I somewhat modified her formula in view of calories, reducing the cheddar and utilizing focus cut bacon. I additionally swapped a portion of the bacon fat for olive oil, yet extremely simply minor changes. The serving of mixed greens was delish, thus fulfilling!

Cleaved SALAD WITH SHRIMP VARIATIONS:

If you don't eat pork, you can swap the bacon for turkey bacon.

To cause this Keto, to discard the corn and include increasingly avocado.

To make this Whole30 or Paleo, preclude the cheddar and corn, include progressively avocado and tomatoes.

You can split this if you're cooking for 1 or twofold to make enough for 4.

This generous Chopped Salad with Shrimp, Avocado, Blue Cheese and Bacon is straightforward and fulfilling. Extraordinary for lunch or supper!

INGREDIENTS

4 cuts focus cut bacon, cleaved

1/2 pound stripped and deveined shrimp

2 cloves garlic, minced

4 ounce margarine lettuce, hacked

1 little corn on the cobb, flame broiled or cooked

1 ounce blue cheddar or gorgonzola

1/2 cup divided cherry tomatoes

2 ounces diced avocado, 1 half little haas

2 teaspoons olive oil genuine salt and dark pepper, to taste

Directions

Warmth a skillet over medium warmth and include the bacon. Cook until fresh and the fat is rendered.

Move the bacon to a paper towel utilizing a slottted spoon.

Expel everything except 1 teaspoon of the bacon oil and dispose of the rest.

Add the shrimp and garlic to the skillet and cook 3 minutes, until dark. Expel and cleave into scaled down pieces.

To gather the serving of mixed greens partition between 2 plates or hurl everything together in an enormous bowl.

Serve immediately, sprinkled with 1 teaspoon olive oil, salt and pepper over every plate of mixed greens.

CHAPTER 7: FREESTYLE MEATLESS RECIPES

MANGO ARUGULA SALAD

Mango avocado and arugula serving of mixed greens

I love the hues in this reviving mango, avocado, and arugula plate of mixed greens with a zesty orange vinaigrette. The blend of arugula, mango, avocado, red onions, cilantro, and red stew peppers make it a fun and brilliant serving of mixed greens. I've generally appreciated plates of mixed greens and am blessed that my children additionally love servings of mixed greens. Particularly the more youthful one, on those days that he chooses to be a meticulous eater (and won't eat the primary dish), he will at present eat his serving of mixed greens and request more. Oddly enough he truly enjoys the onions and can't get enough of them, then he goes for the avocado, next the mango lastly the arugula. To make this serving of mixed greens an increasingly complete feast, you can likewise include flame broiled shrimp, barbecued salmon, or flame broiled chicken.

Servings: For ~ 4 - 6 individuals

Invigorating mango, avocado and arugula plate of mixed greens sprinkled with a zesty orange vinaigrette

Ingredients

6 cups arugula leaves

1 mango, stripped and cut into long cuts

1 avocado, stripped and cut

½ red onion, cut

1 tbs lime juice

For the hot orange vinaigrette

1 tbs champagne vinegar, can likewise utilize juice vinegar or lemon juice

4 tbs squeezed orange, about ½ orange

2 tbs lime juice, about ½ lime

4 tbs olive oil

½ tsp cumin

2 tbs finely cleaved cilantro

1 red bean stew or hot pepper, cut

Salt and pepper

Directions

Consolidate every one of the ingredients for the plate of mixed greens dressing in a container, close it tight and shake until the ingredients are very much blended.

Drench the onion cuts in warm water with a scramble of salt and 1 tbs lime juice for around 10 minutes.

Wash and channel the onions cuts.

Hurl the arugula leaves with half of the vinaigrette.

Include the avocado cuts, mango cuts and onion cuts to the arugula blend, shower the rest of the vinaigrette on top.

Serve right away

CREAM MAYO CORN

Ingredients

4 ears corn

1/2 cup mayonnaise

1/2 cups sharp cream

1/4 cup newly slashed cilantro leaves

1 cup newly ground Parmesan

1 lime, squeezed

Red stew powder, to taste

2 limes cut into wedges, for embellish

Bearings

Expel the husks of the corn however leave the center joined toward the end so you have something to clutch. Flame broil the corn on a hot barbecue or cast iron frying pan skillet until somewhat scorched. Turn it so it gets cooked equally everywhere. Blend the mayonnaise, sharp cream and cilantro together. Mesh the Parmesan in another bowl. While the corn is still warm slather with mayonnaise blend. Press lime squeeze over the corn and shower with Parmesan. Season with stew powder and present with additional lime wedges.

EGGS GREEN BEAN SALAD

This simple plate of mixed greens is a gently dressed with a tomato juice and vinegar blend, and the cut hard-bubbled eggs give it additional protein and flavor. Serve the plate of mixed greens on lettuce leaves, arugula, infant spinach or kale, or blended serving of mixed greens.

Ingredients

2 cups solidified French-cut beans (around 12 to 16 ounces)

1 tablespoon juice vinegar

1/4 cup tomato juice or V-8 juice

2 teaspoons granulated sugar

1/4 teaspoon dried leaf tarragon (disintegrated, or dried leaf basil)

1 tablespoon finely minced or ground red or yellow onion

3 tablespoon cleaved pimiento salt and crisply ground dark pepper (to taste)

2 hard-cooked eggs (cut) lettuce leaves or blended serving of mixed greens

Steps to Make It

Cook the green beans following bundle headings. Channel well and move to a bowl.

In a screw-top container, join the tomato squeeze, sugar, and disintegrated tarragon or basil. Shake to mix completely. Put in a safe spot.

Add the onion and pimiento to the green beans. Hurl with the dressing.

Line four plates with lettuce leaves. Partition the cut hard-bubbled eggs equally among the plates, and afterward top with the green bean blend.

Sprinkle each serving softly with salt and newly ground dark pepper.

FETA CHICKPEA SALAD

All on board the new express! It's the ideal opportunity for Mediterranean Chickpea Salad. This is straightforward chickpea serving of mixed greens is uplifting, filling, and one of my outright most loved dinners to have sitting tight in my cooler for sound snacks. It tastes fab at room temperature, making it a MVP formula for potlucks and evening gatherings. Regardless of what the climate is doing outside, it places me in a late spring perspective.

Made with chime peppers all things considered, new herbs, fresh cucumber, and velvety feta, each chomp tastes of warm, radiant minutes. Protein-and fiber-rich chickpeas make it a healthy veggie lover principle, or you can serve it as a simple side with chicken, fish, or shrimp.

This Mediterranean Chickpea Salad is a formula I as a rule put something aside for summer, however I found myself needing it relentlessly not long ago.

I additionally got myself "contributing" a not-insignificant piece of my early evening time investigating flights from Milwaukee to [insert warm climate goal here] absent a lot of karma. Happenstance? The thermometer proposes not.

If you are longing for a new break as much as I am, give this Mediterranean Chickpea Salad formula a turn. It probably won't be an outing to the sea shore, yet it will light up your day more than you anticipate.

We've been eating a considerable measure of overwhelming solace food of late, so I was enchanted by how much making something lighter livened up my evening... and I was significantly increasingly pleased to have the scraps taken care of my cooler for quick, solid dinners on request!

My Favorite Mediterranean Chickpea Salad

This simple chickpea plate of mixed greens is one of those wonderful no-cook suppers that scarcely needs a formula. Like this chickpea plate of mixed greens sandwich and chickpea fish serving of mixed greens, it makes the best of wash room staples (hello there, chickpeas) and new ingredients.

The new ingredients are ones I often partner with the Mediterranean (and the great Greek serving of mixed greens from my preferred Mediterranean eatery back home).

Ringer peppers. Sweet, vivid crunch.

Fresh cucumber. Each time I eat it, I wonder why I don't have it all the more often. It makes each feast you serve it with taste new. This Cucumber Tomato Avocado Salad is another most loved cucumber dish.

Velvety feta cheddar. Best things in life.

Parsley. Crisp herbs like parsley are a little expansion that have a major effect. It gives this chickpea serving of mixed greens a total, cleaned taste you'd miss without it.

The chickpea serving of mixed greens dressing is a 30-second red wine vinaigrette that you can shake together right in a bricklayer container. Showy overhead pour discretionary however energized.

The different genuine ingredient star here is chickpeas. They're high in fiber and protein, cheap, and staggeringly flexible.

You can utilize chickpeas for burgers (like these Mediterranean Quinoa Burgers), in a hot chickpea serving of mixed greens (like this Moroccan Chickpea Salad—it's an extraordinary, warm zesty versus a consume your-mouth hot fiery).

You can likewise eat chickpeas from the can, however I'm trusting you'll make things a stride further and consolidate them with new ingredients to make this Mediterranean Chickpea Salad!

Approaches to Serve Chickpea Salad

Appreciate it all alone, directly out of the bowl. The chickpeas make it bounty filling for a light and stunning dinner.

If you needed to up the veggies considerably more, you could prepare this chickpea serving of mixed greens with crisp greens (arugula is my top choice), then extra a touch of additional dressing to make a green plate of mixed greens.

Chickpea plate of mixed greens with avocado. Include huge pieces of crisp avocado and split cherry tomatoes for extra servings of solid fats and vivid veggies.

Chickpea Salad Pitas. Stuff it inside warmed, split entire wheat pita bread.

FETA CORN TREAT

Ingredients

1 cup pecans

4 cups new corn bits (from 4 ears), crude or cooked

2 jalapenos, seeded and daintily cut

2 tablespoons new lime juice

2 tablespoons extra-virgin olive oil legitimate salt and dark pepper

1/2 cup disintegrated Feta (2 ounces

Step by step instructions to Make It

Stage 1

Warmth broiler to 400° F. Spread the pecans on a rimmed preparing sheet and toast until fragrant, 6 to 8 minutes. Let cool and generally hack.

Stage 2

In a huge bowl, join the corn, jalapeños, lime juice, oil, pecans, 1/2 teaspoon salt, and 1/4 teaspoon pepper. Sprinkle with the Feta before serving.

MARINARA BROCCOLI MEAL

INGREDIENTS

2 teaspoons olive oil

2 teaspoons minced garlic

1 14.5-ounce can diced tomatoes in tomato puree, Italian-style, if accessible

1 pound broccoli florets, around 5 cups

1/4 cup Parmesan cheddar, destroyed pepper, to taste

Directions

Warmth oil in a huge, secured, nonstick skillet over medium warmth. Include garlic and sauté for a moment or two, blending continually.

Pour in the diced tomatoes with puree and cook around five minutes (lessen warmth to medium-low, if required, to keep it at a delicate bubble).

Spot the broccoli over the tomatoes and season with pepper. Spread skillet and stew over low heat for five minutes. Sprinkle Parmesan over the top, spread skillet once more, and keep cooking until broccoli is delicate (around 4 minutes more). Try not to overcook the broccoli; it ought to be an energetic green. Fill in as seems to be, or hurl the broccoli with the marinara sauce and appreciate!

ARUGULA GREENS SALAD

This plate of mixed greens is an adjustment of one I've been making as of late for companions when facilitating. It's so basic in nature you likely as of now have a large portion of the ingredients close by the present moment (the best sort of formula, as I would like to think).

Peppery arugula is joined with fresh apples, toasted walnuts, red onion, and dried cranberries, and it's everything dressed with a splendid, energetic lemon vinaigrette.

Furthermore, only 15 minutes (!!) and 8 essential ingredients to plan – my concept of plate of mixed greens flawlessness.

This would make the ideal light and sound dish to assist you with topping off on plants and eradicate a portion of that pie coerce likely waiting from yesterday's banquet. We've all been there. Serving of mixed greens to the salvage.

Presently, life.

This season, everybody guides you to be grateful for what you have. I concur. Slow down, be thankful – it's useful for the spirit.

However, shouldn't something be said about when life is hard, or things don't go the manner in which you arranged, or something occurs and your feeling of reality shifts? What then?

2015 was maybe my most specifically testing year yet, one wherein things turned out poorly 'anticipated' me. I was left feeling somewhat dismal and irate and baffled and just for the most dislike myself (what an unusual sensation). Everything caused me to acknowledge I'm not as solid or unconstrained or flexible as I suspected I seemed to be. To put it plainly, this year sort of beat me down.

The lumpy subtleties aren't the significant part. The significant part is I believe it's OK to be pitiful, or furious, or baffled, or tired, or whatever it is you're feeling right well that is not brilliant bliss. It doesn't mean you're not appreciative. It just means you're giving yourself consent to feel your sentiments (which is alive and well, incidentally). What's more, it's OK if what turns out isn't all roses and daylight.

My support is, deal with it if you have to. Nobody's looking at any rate. And keeping in mind that you're busy, eat some pie and embrace your mother. I've seen these as similarly adequate cures.

Ingredients

US Customary - Metric

Serving of mixed greens

1/2 cup crude walnuts

7 ounces arugula (natural when conceivable)

2 little apples (1 tart, 1 sweet/stripped, quartered, cored and meagerly cut the long way)

1/4 red onion (meagerly cut)

2 Tbsp dried cranberries (discretionary)

DRESSING

1 enormous lemon, squeezed (1 lemon yields ~3 Tbsp or 45 ml)

1 Tbsp maple syrup

1 squeeze every ocean salt + dark pepper

3 Tbsp olive oil

Guidelines

Preheat broiler to 350 degrees F (176 C) and organize walnuts on an uncovered preparing sheet.

Heat walnuts for 8-10 minutes or until fragrant and profound brilliant dark colored. Expel from broiler and put in a safe spot.

While walnuts are toasting, prep remaining serving of mixed greens ingredients and add to an enormous blending bowl.

Plan dressing in a blending bowl or artisan container by including all ingredients and whisking or shaking overwhelmingly to join. Taste and modify enhance as required.

Add walnuts to plate of mixed greens and top with dressing. Hurl to join and serve right away. Serves two as an entrée and 4 as a side (as unique formula is composed/change if adjusting clump size).

Store remains (dressing separate from plate of mixed greens) shrouded in the cooler for 2-3 days (however best when new). Dressing should keep at room temperature for 2-3 days when all around fixed.

EGG MAYO SALAD

My family is brimming with egg sweethearts so we love this astonishing egg serving of mixed greens. Indeed my sweet sister disclosed to me that she made this formula multiple times in a single week. For best outcomes cooking and stripping hard bubbled ensure you take a gander at my supportive insights on the most proficient method to make impeccable hard bubbled eggs.

HOW DO YOU MAKE CREAMY EGG SALAD RECIPE?

First hard-heat up your eggs ensuring that you pursue my basic hints on making impeccable hard-bubbled eggs. Then just strip them and coarsely slash. Finely slash the red pepper and meagerly cut the celery. Then consolidate the eggs, mayonnaise, Dijon mustard, red pepper, celery and squashed red pepper and mix delicately. Include salt and newly ground dark pepper to taste.

The most effective method to MAKE PERFECT HARD BOILED EGGS

I have hard bubbled handfuls and many eggs throughout the years. There are a few stages to effectively cooking hard bubbled eggs.

Picking THE RIGHT EGGS

You need eggs that are as near lapse as could be allowed. Not terminated yet close. Some of the time the Mom and Pop supermarkets have them as turnover isn't as high as the chain distribution centers and markets. This is by a long shot the most significant moment that it comes to stripping them effectively.

COOKING THE HARD BOILED EGGS

Add the eggs to a huge pot without congestion. Fill the pot with cold water to an inch over the eggs, Add one teaspoon of preparing pop. Next carry the eggs to a delicate bubble. Then put the cover on the dish and expel it from the warmth. Enable the eggs to sit in the dish undisturbed for twelve to fifteen minutes. I utilize twelve minutes for the medium eggs and fifteen minutes for the large eggs. Expel the dish from the stove and spot under freezing running water for a few minutes. The eggs should feel freezing before you shut the water off. At last let them sit in the driving rain water for an extra fifteen to twenty minutes. Store in the cooler

Approaches TO ENJOY EGG SALAD!

Serve egg plate of mixed greens for informal breakfast or a light super.

Spoon on multi grain wraps and daintily toasted entire wheat or sourdough bread.

For a difference in pace stuff in a sun-matured tomato or avocado.

Keep it very solid and spoon over a bed of spring greens.

For additional crunch server on crostini.

Appreciate with melba toast or fresh light saltines

CHAPTER 8: FREESTYLE DESSERTS

BLUEBERRY LEMON MUFFINS

Lemon Blueberry Muffins look and suggest a flavor like something out of an extravagant pastry shop yet far and away superior because you get the opportunity to eat them warm thus new out of the stove. That lemon coat over the top is "discretionary, yet exceptionally important." My goodness my is it great!

This biscuit formula couldn't be simpler – both the blueberry biscuits and the sweet lemon coat. I scored significant focuses with my family and they ate up these rapidly. They are fabulous with a major cup of tea or espresso and the coating make these totally overwhelming and shocking for summer early lunch parties. Everything about these is great.

Ingredients for Blueberry Muffins:

Cook's Tip: Measuring accurately in preparing is everything! Watch our top tips and deceives on the most proficient method to quantify ingredients precisely.

This blueberry biscuits formula is so basic and the way to progress isn't to over-blend in the wake of beating the eggs and sugar. You need to see modest knots in the player in the wake of blending in the flour and it ought not be consummately smooth. I utilized an electric hand blender to beat the eggs and sugar then included the flour, pizzazz and lemon juice with a whisk lastly collapsed in the blueberries with a spatula.

Calories: 319 kcal

Servings: 12 biscuits

Ingredients

Ingredients for Blueberry Muffins:

2 eggs (enormous), room temperature

1 cup granulated sugar

1 cup acrid cream

1/2 cup additional LIGHT olive oil not additional virgin

1 tsp vanilla extricate

1/4 tsp ocean salt

2 cups generally useful flour *measured accurately

2 tsp preparing powder

2 tsp lemon get-up-and-go from 1 huge lemon

2 Tbsp lemon juice from 1 huge lemon

1/2 cups new blueberries washed and dried

Discretionary (yet profoundly essential) Lemon Glaze Recipe:

1 cup powdered sugar

1/2 Tbsp new lemon juice (utilize 1/2 to 2 Tbsp)

1/2 tsp lemon get-up-and-go

US Customary - Metric

Directions

Instructions to Make Blueberry Muffins Recipe:

Line a 12-check biscuit/cupcake tin with cupcake liners. Preheat stove to 400°F. In a huge blending bowl, beat together 2 eggs and 1 cup granulated sugar with electric blender on fast 5 minutes. It ought to be thick and light in shading.

Include 1 cup sharp cream, 1/2 cup oil, 1 tsp vanilla and 1/4 tsp salt. Set the blender to low speed and blend just until joined.

In a little bowl, include 2 cups flour and 2 tsp heating powder and rush to consolidate. Utilizing a hand held whisk, include flour blend into the hitter 1/3 at once, mixing with every expansion just until fused. Don't OVERMIX or biscuits can get thick.

Include 2 tsp lemon pizzazz 2 Tbsp lemon squeeze and rush in just until consolidated. Utilize a spatula to overlay in 1/2 cups blueberries, collapsing just until consolidated.

Separation player into biscuit tin filling liners to the top or until the entirety of the hitter is spent. Prepare at 400°F for 20-22 minutes or until tops are brilliant and a toothpick embedded into the middle tell the truth without wet batter. Expel biscuits from tin and cool on a wire rack until room temperature then sprinkle with lemon coat.

Instructions to Make Lemon Glaze Recipe:

In a little bowl, consolidate 1 cup powdered sugar, 1/2 tsp lemon pizzazz and 1/2 to 2 Tbsp lemon juice, including lemon juice until wanted consistency is come to. Mix until smooth. To thin the coating more, include a little lemon squeeze or water. To thicken, include somewhat more powdered sugar.

APPLESAUCE BEAN BROWNIES

Those simple Vegan Black Bean Brownies fruit purée improved have NO additional sugar ! They are the solid chocolate pastries you need right now ! It is low calorie, low carb and gluten free with a heavenly chocolate fudgy surface. If you watch the carbs, a cut contains just 5 gram carbs and 3 g of protein for each serve to keep you full for more. So continue perusing for the formula !

Along these lines, those veggie lover dark bean brownies fruit purée improved are the fudgiest brownie ever! Since I am attempting to diminish eggs in preparing I found astounding elective like unsweetened fruit purée. I purchase a natural fruit purée which contains 9 g of common sugar per 100 g. All that sugar is originating from the apple just which is an incredible solid choice to improve those brownie. In addition, fruit purée include an extra fudgy surface that I totally love.

I utilized stevia dim chocolate in the formula – it is a 100% sugar free chocolate made of cocoa powder and improved with stevia. It is extraordinary if you need to maintain a strategic distance from extra carbs/sugar in a formula however keep it sweet. It dissolve splendidly, it is low calories and give a delightful sweet taste without including sugar. As those vegetarian dark beans brownies serve 16 squares one piece contains just 5 g of carbs and a little measure of 1.4 g sugar – it is a fourth of teaspoon of characteristic sugar from apples. Stunning right?

FUDGY, LOW CALORIES AND ONLY 6 INGREDIENTS

I am dependent on veggie lover brownies ! Truly, veggie lover brownies are the best. WHY? I understood that egg free brownies are not so much chewy but rather more fudgy. My fudgy date brownies was my first preliminary, and this second veggie lover brownie with dark bean and fruit purée affirm my thought! Furthermore, dark beans are a stunning wellspring of protein and iron so healthfully you won't miss your eggs. I prescribe a food processor to make this formula yet all you need are 6 rudiments ingredients:

Dark beans – I utilized canned dark beans, flushed and depleted

Almond feast – additionally know as ground almond

Unsweetened fruit purée – I utilized natural fruit purée yet it works with custom made fruit purée as well

Dull chocolate – I made this formula with sugar free stevia chocolate and I additionally tried 85% cooca or 70% cocoa. Everything works impeccably. The darker chocolate you use, the severe the brownie will be.

Coconut oil

Heating powder

It is discretionary however you can likewise include 1 teaspoon of vanilla pith in this formula. I generally figure we should include additional vanilla in heating. I simply love it. So now take a gander at this fudgy surface, isn't that stunning?

If you are a brownie sweetheart as I do, yet don't have any desire to enjoy on an excessively sweet or calories stacked brownie, attempt this one! You will cherish it. For an extra fudgy surface, store this in the cooler, you will love it! Appreciate.

PUMPKIN CAKE MUFFINS

This two ingredient pumpkin biscuit formula is one of those. When the children have companions over, or for a speedy hot breakfast, this is immaculate! Indeed, this is simple formula telling you the best way to make pumpkin biscuits utilizing cake blend.

Pumpkin biscuits have two ingredients. It appears pointless excess to do the bit by bit yet why not! The primary concern is, get your preferred red bowl and your preferred spoon. Do you have a most loved spoon? Here is mine:

These biscuits are so too brisk!

Biscuit making tip!

Utilize a scoop to place the mixture into the biscuit wells. Flawlessly assigned and less chaotic!!

Track with bit by bit and at the base of this formula is the printable variant. Here's the straightforward on the most proficient method to make pumpkin biscuits with zest cake blend! Beneath this is the printable formula.

Ingredients:

1 zest cake blend

1 can 15 or 16 oz pumpkin puree (little can, not pie filling)

Headings

Preheat broiler to 325 degrees.

Combine zest cake blend in with pumpkin. Scoop into lined or well-showered biscuits.

Heat 18-20 minutes (until toothpick confesses all).

Be cautioned, the children do like them.

CHAPTER 9: BASICS OF RAPID WEIGHT LOSS

If you've chosen to attempt Rapid weight loss, there are a few different participation alternatives to look over – including an advanced just choice, a gathering meeting choice, and a customized training choice. Every one of the three offer a similar essential program; it's just the additional responsibility and bolster that differs between them.

On the eating regimen, you can hope to follow your foods day by day and remain inside a specified scope of Points. No foods are untouchable, and as long as you eat inside your focuses spending plan every day – you'll likely lose weight. However, a few people do find that the steady following and spotlight on the scale can get troublesome.

What to Eat

Rapid weight loss has developed impressively since its initiation in the 1960's. As of now, the Rapid Weight Loss Freestyle program offers a ton of adaptability for agreeable foods when following the program, and there are no foods that are specifically prohibited. There are a few foods that will in general be exceptionally high in focuses, however, which you'll have to restrict.

Agreeable Foods:

Products of the soil – Produce has consistently been indispensable to the Rapid weight loss program, even in its underlying trade framework. Pretty much every new products of the soil (with a couple of exemptions, similar to potatoes and avocados) check in at zero, bumping those following the program to top off on these supplement thick decisions.

Poultry and Seafood – Though a wide range of poultry and seafood are permitted, inclination is given to lean proteins like skinless chicken bosom, turkey bosom, and fish – which are all zero points. Different meats can be incorporated routinely in the eating regimen inside the Points recompense.

Beans and Lentils – As of the 2017 Rapid Weight Loss Freestyle update, all beans and lentils are currently viewed as zero points. These foods are an incredible mix of sound sugars, fiber, and protein, making them a superb expansion to your plate.

Eggs – Though eggs were at first constrained in early varieties of Rapid weight loss, they're at present supported. Truth be told, eggs are presently a zero point food, so appreciate some mixed up with veggies for breakfast or add a hardboiled egg to your mid-evening nibble.

Dairy – All dairy is permitted on Rapid weight loss, however your frozen yogurt will absolutely cost a larger number of focuses than a glass of skim milk. Plain unsweetened yogurt is zero, however, so join it with crisp organic product for a sound tidbit that won't consume your point complete.

Grains – There's space for all grains on Rapid Weight Loss Freestyle, from dark colored rice to quinoa to amaranth. All grains have point esteems, so make certain to work them into your day by day allowance.

Resistant Foods:

Actually any food can fit into the Rapid Weight Loss Freestyle plan. In any case, some might be so high in Points that it is difficult to suit them into your routine consistently. The vast majority of these are foods or parts that should just be expended every so often in any case in the domain of in general smart dieting.

Suggested Timing

There's no official dinner plan while on Rapid weight loss. The vast majority do well on a standard eating plan, expending three suppers per day with a tidbit or two in between.

Despite the fact that you have a financial limit of focuses, you ought to likewise attempt to focus on your inward craving and completion prompts when thinking about how to time your dinners. Eat when genuinely eager and stop when you are easily fulfilled.

Assets and Tips

Program Options and Costs:

If you choose to utilize the Rapid weight loss plan, you'll look over one of three paid options:

Advanced – Provides your Points remittance and awards you access to the online application to follow your foods. Expenses around $3 to $7 every week, contingent upon the length of responsibility and any uncommon offers.

Workshop – Allows access to the computerized segments and furthermore incorporates into individual gathering gatherings. Expenses around $5 to $9 every week, contingent upon the length of responsibility and any unique offers.

Instructing – Includes everything in the other two projects, and furthermore incorporates one-on-one help from a customized mentor. Expenses around $9 to $14 every week, contingent upon the length of responsibility and any unique offers

Accommodating Tips:

Regardless of which program you pick, here are a couple of accommodating tips:

Download the Rapid weight loss application to effectively follow your Points. The application enables you to rapidly scan for foods, add them to your every day food log, and access day in and day out visit support. You'll additionally have the option to utilize it to compute Points for dinners that you eat out.

Capitalize on your zero points foods by incorporating them in dinners and tidbits. These foods are commonly low in calories and plentiful in nutrients, minerals, fiber, or protein. For instance, if you typically make a pan fried food with generally pork and rice, change things up to be for the most part vegetables (zero points) with littler measures of poultry and rice.

Say something week by week. Despite the fact that not all specialists concur with regular weigh-ins, numerous different experts do bolster this Rapid weight loss occupant. Saying something week after week assists individuals with following patterns on the scale. You can tip the scales at home or at the in-person gatherings (don't stress, gauge ins are done secretly and not before the gathering). Seeing a couple of pounds dropped can give you the proceeded with inspiration you have to stay with the program.

Exercise consistently. In spite of the fact that you can get more fit without working out, remaining fit will help with your general health all through life. Rapid weight loss urges you to procure Points by remaining dynamic.

Modifications

Because there are no beyond reach foods, Rapid weight loss is quite simple to modify to meet your requirements. For instance, if you're not an aficionado of meat, you can without much of a stretch fuse beans or tofu in your supper plan. If you're lactose-narrow minded, you can search for sans lactose dairy choices or options that fit your Points balance.

Be that as it may, there are a couple of gatherings for whom Rapid weight loss restricts use (and for good reason):9

Pregnant ladies

People with a dietary problem

Youngsters under 18

Likewise, while those with a BMI of 18.5 or under may join Rapid weight loss, they are not allowed to set a weight reduction objective.

Rapid weight loss does right now offer a program for teenagers, which has been dubious in the sustenance world. They do necessitate that the high schooler falls at the 95th percentile or above on the BMI graph, and a marked specialist's note that gives them authorization to participate.

Moreover, individuals with diabetes may require extra direction while following Rapid weight loss. For instance, however products of the soil are zero point foods, they still most certainly affect glucose levels. If you have diabetes, meet with a dietitian to talk about your individual needs (which can be joined with Rapid weight loss if wanted).

Regardless of whether you don't have any contraindications to taking part in Rapid weight loss, recollect that the program isn't for everybody. If any eating routine turns out to be excessively prohibitive and prompts misery, it might be a sign that you ought to pick a different eating plan. For certain individuals, however, Rapid weight loss can offer the perfect measure of structure to help their objectives.

CHAPTER 10:
ADVANTAGES AND
DISADVANTAGES OF
RAPID WEIGHT LOSS

Rapid weight loss is a prominent eating regimen that assists individuals with shedding pounds through its point-tallying framework. You're required to follow your food admission (as every food has a doled out point worth) and remain inside your day by day focuses spending plan. Since fatty or void calorie foods utilize more focuses, constraining those will diminish your general vitality admission and assist you with shedding pounds.

This doesn't mean the arrangement is the correct decision for everybody, however. While Rapid weight loss has its positive properties, it additionally may prompt undesirable abstaining from excessive food intake propensities. A few people feel the steady following is unsavory, and others may control focuses, (for example, skipping dinners to bank focuses for less solid foods). It likewise can be exorbitant after some time.

Aces

Adjusted and adaptable

Shows lifelong aptitudes

No foods are illegal

Gradual weight reduction

Huge amounts of help and assets

Decreases diabetes hazard

Advances work out

Cons

Can be exorbitant

Tallying focuses can be repetitive

Week after week weigh-ins are essential

Constrained proof for cardiovascular benefits

An excess of opportunity for certain individuals

May prompt unfortunate eating fewer carbs

Geniuses

Adjusted and Flexible

Rapid weight loss offers one of the most adaptable business consumes less calories available. By doling out vegetables, organic products, and lean proteins an estimation of zero, the eating routine urges you to make these the main part of your suppers while as yet taking into consideration sufficient grains and dairy inside your day by day Points portion.

Shows Lifelong Skills

Regardless of what diet plan you pick, you need it to be something you can pursue forever. Rapid weight loss shows basic good dieting abilities that will work well for you after some time - like estimating your segments and serving sizes and urging you to prepare food at home.

No Foods are Forbidden

There is no rundown of foods to stay away from on Rapid weight loss like you'll discover on different eating regimens. Rather, you'll tally Points and gain Points. The point framework urges you to eat well food yet in addition enables you to enjoy with sweet treats or snacks now and again.

Gradual Weight Loss

You can hope to lose one to two pounds per week on Rapid weight loss. A few studies have bolstered these cases and demonstrated the program to be powerful for weight reduction.

For instance, one investigation distributed in 2017 in Lancet thought about weight reduction among those utilizing self-improvement materials, Rapid weight loss for 12 weeks, or Rapid weight loss for 52 weeks. The 52-week program prompted preferred outcomes over the 12-week program, and the 12-week program would be advised to results than the independently directed program.1

Another 2015 methodical survey in Annals of inner drug analyzed a few business health improvement plans. The investigation found that those on Rapid weight loss lost 2.6 percent more weight contrasted with control groups.2

Strangely, a far reaching influence may likewise exist for companions of those taking an interest in Rapid weight loss (or other health improvement plans). A study distributed in 2018 in Obesity discovered significant weight reduction among companions of those partaking in Rapid weight loss, despite the fact that they themselves didn't join.3

Huge amounts of Support and Resources

Rapid weight loss offers a larger number of assets than most other eating regimen programs. You'll discover the application and site convenient for figuring and following Points, just as discovering formula thoughts.

If you like responsibility and gathering support, you can likewise go to the ordinary gathering gatherings. You can even pursue a top notch participation that incorporates customized training for one-on-one help.

Additionally, if you claim a Fitbit for weight reduction, or utilize another gadget or weight reduction application like Jawbone, Withings, Misfit, Garmin Vivofit, Apple Health, or Map-My-Run, you can adjust your action to Rapid weight loss. This encourages you deal with all your physical action and weight reduction information in one spot.

Decreases Diabetes Risk

Because Rapid weight loss steers clients towards nutritious choices and assists individuals with getting in shape, the program has been related with a diminished danger of type 2 diabetes or better glucose control among those with diabetes.

For instance, an investigation distributed in 2017 in BMJ open diabetes inquire about and care took a gander at the impacts of alluding those with pre-diabetes to a free Rapid weight loss program. The individuals who took an interest shed pounds and decreased hemoglobin A1c levels (a proportion of glucose control). Indeed, 38 percent of patients came back to totally typical blood glucose metrics.4

Different studies have discovered comparative outcomes among those with pre-diabetes, incorporating a study distributed in BMJ Open Diabetes Research and Care in 2017.5 Another study distributed in 2016 in Obesity (Silver Springs) has likewise indicated the individuals who as of now have diabetes experienced weight reduction and better glucose control when following the Rapid weight loss program.6

Advances Exercise

The Rapid weight loss framework empowers a lot of every day development and exercise. You procure Points with development that assist you with offsetting your food consumption. Direction is accommodated new exercisers and for the individuals who can work out more earnestly and consume more calories.

Despite the fact that there are numerous advantages to Rapid weight loss, that doesn't mean it's an ideal choice for everybody. Think about the disadvantages before putting resources into the arrangement.

Cons

Can Be Costly

The expense for Rapid weight loss will fluctuate from individual to individual, contingent upon the choices you select and to what extent you'd like to remain on the program. Make certain to consider the absolute expense for the whole time you should be on the arrangement to ensure that you can manage the cost of it.

Computerized just writing computer programs is the least expensive alternative, while in-person workshops fall in the center, and customized instructing will cost the most. Current prices run from around $4 every week on the low end for the online program, to around $14 every week for customized instructing.

You can get somewhat limited week by week rates by paying in advance for a while, or by watching out for advancements. Some medical coverage organizations likewise offer a rebate for Rapid weight loss, so make certain to check with yours if you're wanting to join.

Exactly what amount does it cost all things considered for individuals to arrive at their objectives? In an examination that investigated the expense for a gathering of ladies to lose 5 percent of their body weight, they discovered Rapid weight loss checked in at roughly $1,610. While this may seem like a ton, think about the cost-reserve funds that may come later with better in general wellbeing. Likewise, this sum was still far not exactly the other health improvement plan considered, Curves Complete, which checked in at $8,613 to accomplish similar objectives.

Checking Points Can Be Tedious

If you don't care for checking calories, you dislike tallying Points either. The procedure can be tedious and might be unreasonably muddled for individuals who need a fast and basic way to deal with eating.

Week after week Weigh-Ins Are Necessary

You have to say something once per week to keep tabs on your development on Rapid weight loss. For certain individuals, this necessity is awkward. You dislike to be tipped the scales at a gathering meeting (despite the fact that the say something just happens before the pioneer, not the whole gathering). Or on the other hand you may get disappointed by absence of progress on the scale that week, despite the fact that you pursued your arrangement exactly.

For other people, however, week after week weigh-ins can be an or more, observing advancement and remain progressing nicely.

Restricted Evidence for Cardiovascular Benefits

A deliberate audit in 2016 found that Rapid weight loss offered minimal extra help for pulse or cholesterol contrasted with control gatherings – however information was limited. If you're searching for an eating regimen with set up cardiovascular benefits, you might need to examine different alternatives (like the Mediterranean diet, for instance).

An excessive amount of Freedom

As senseless as it sounds, an excessive amount of opportunity can be an Achilles heel for certain individuals. The capacity to pick anything you need to eat may demonstrate excessively enticing. It is totally conceivable to utilize all your Points on not exactly nutritious foods. If that addresses your character, weight reduction plans with stricter rules may work better.

May Lead to Unhealthy Dieting

There is some worry that the emphasis on tallying focuses can prompt an undesirable association with food. For instance, there have been narrative reports that some Rapid weight loss adherents "set aside" focuses to gorge on food later. In spite of the fact that they may not surpass their day by day focuses, that conduct does breech on undesirable consuming less calories.

You Can Earn points on Rapid weight loss

Rapid weight loss empowers every day exercise and general physical action by giving you points with development regularly. There is direction given to assist you with adjusting your physical action and food admission so you benefit from your Rapid weight loss experience.

Slow and Steady

Last, however not least, you'll get thinner at a gradual pace which means you'll be progressively well-suited to keep the weight off when you use Rapid weight loss and your eating routine plan. While you may lose more weight from the outset, as your body alters, you'll for the most part lose one to two pounds for each week on Rapid weight loss.

Cons of Rapid weight loss

Here you're keen on the upsides and downsides of Rapid weight loss then here are the not all that constructive parts, in spite of the fact that I's still 100% prescribe this weight reduction plan as I for one believe it's well justified, despite all the trouble.

Rapid weight loss May Be Expensive

You'll need to pay a month to month charge to be a Rapid weight loss part. This can get costly for those with a tight family spending plan.

Fortunately there are a couple of different Rapid weight loss intends to be a piece of, enabling you to pick a choice most appropriate for your spending limit. You should go to month to month gatherings or you can choose an online rendition.

If you're yet to choose, you might need to visit the Free Rapid weight loss adding machine and try the arrangement out for a week or so before you purchase.

The uplifting news is Rapid weight loss often have free preliminaries or rebate codes to help make joining less expensive.

Rapid weight loss Weekly Weigh-in

Rapid weight loss Weekly weigh-ins are required as a major aspect of the Rapid weight loss program. This can be awkward for certain individuals. Being said something front of others can be very humiliating if you're not into having other individuals know your advancement or absence of progress.

Fortunately when you are said something a gathering, this should be possible circumspectly. Your outcomes won't be yelled out from the rooftop tops and if you're following the online arrangement you can say something from the solace of your own home.

An excess of Freedom On Rapid weight loss

While having the option to eat anything you need while on Rapid weight loss might be engaging a few people, for other people, it might be an excess of opportunity.

With a lot of opportunity to eat what you wish during this eating routine arrangement, you may end up gorging or as yet picking off base food alternatives to lose the most weight.

Be that as it may if you plan sound suppers, use rapid weight loss cook books, pick a lot of solid zero points foods and search for tasty depressed spot plans you can truly keep up a decent diet and take advantage of your Rapid weight loss venture.

There you have it, the huge rundown of the advantages and disadvantages of Rapid weight loss. At last the choice is yours with respect to what diet plan you pick, however in any case, we would all be able to concur that figuring out how to get thinner and feel more beneficial is a decent objective to have in life.

CHAPTER 11: WHY RAPID WEIGHT LOSS LEAVES YOU FEELING LIKE A DISAPPOINTMENT

Stories like this are so unsurprising and regular because diets cause our bodies to respond in specific manners and our psyches to stall out in certain idea designs – the two of which that are NOT what you are searching for.

Physically, confinement (which means not eating to fulfillment, not simply eating what you THINK is sufficient) causes a great deal of anguish

Basic hunger

Pigging out

Distraction with food because your body believes it's in a starvation!!

Rationally confinement causes a great deal of issues too.

This distraction with food diverts us from our lives and it winds up being all we're considering!

We become restless, over the top, blameworthy and embarrassed when we surrender to everything, unavoidably.

ANY program that cutoff points food in any capacity – food gathering, calories, sums and so on is an eating routine.

Continuously.

Inevitably.

No exemptions.

Diets, for example,

Keto, entire 30 – these are truly clear as crystal, they limit food gatherings, straightforward enough.

Be that as it may, shouldn't something be said about discontinuous fasting, macros and Rapid Weight Loss Program? These in fact enable you to eat anything you desire. Be that as it may, isn't that right? NO – there are consistently confinements.

Furthermore, restrictions mean weight control plans.

So how Might we identify an eating regimen when it appears to be iffy?

(Numerous organizations are receiving IE language so now and again it really can be precarious)

Signs to pay special mind to:

Any notice of gauging or weight reduction

Constraints around a specific foods, food gatherings, timing of eating., ANYTHING

Any discussion around THIS being "the way". There is literally nothing that works for everybody (other than tuning in to YOUR own assortment obviously).

Any numbers – calories, weight, macros, and so forth

Notice of mending your association with food/finishing voraciously consuming food without looking at expecting to quit limiting.

Finally, the attitudes that these weight control plans get you in is truly what keeps you stuck in the cycle and making it HARD to get out.

These attitudes are:

1. Win big or bust reasoning

This is the mentality that stalls out in the cycle

Tallying your focuses flawlessly all week just to go insane after your say something

It is possible that you're being impeccable or saying screw it

How might we start getting away from this outlook?

Think about day by day where you could have everything.

Might you be able to go to the rec center AND join your companions for pizza today still?

Might you be able to have that serving of mixed greens yet its alright to skirt the exercise center, you're so worn out!

Might you be able to have two or three your mothers treats and afterward proceed onward with your day regularly?

Starting to see where you can make more recurring pattern in your day by day life will move you towards having the option to have everything and escape the cycle for good.

2. Considering food positive or negative

This is the thing that we were shown our entire lives.

So it's absolutely ordinary to think along these lines yet heres the thing...

A large number of us think as increasingly nutritious and less nutritious foods as fortunate or unfortunate yet that brings profound quality into it.

You aren't great if you eat your veggies and terrible if you have dessert yet that is actually how diet culture capacities.

This brings blame and disgrace for eating which prompts gorging and the win big or bust cycle once more.

Rapid weight loss at long last lost the "weight."

The organization that is spent the greater part a century helping individuals thin somewhere near making a care group (and food focuses framework) to enable them to watch what they eat is the most recent brand understanding that people are increasingly started up to grasp wellbeing over weight reduction.

It not just rebranded itself as " Rapid Weight Loss " on Monday, but at the same time it's collaborated with the Headspace reflection application to get its 4.6 million individuals around the globe chipping away at care. In addition, the Rapid Weight Loss application is being patched up to get clients following sound propensities like keeping food journals, moving their bodies and going to Rapid Weight Loss occasions in return for remunerations focuses that they can exchange for Rapid Weight Loss marked merchandise and encounters

"Individuals are changing ... the period of abstaining from excessive food intake was about society forcing what you 'should' resemble, and individuals revealing to you what to eat. What's more, presently we are moving into a period of health," Gail Tifford, the main brand official from Rapid weight loss, told Moneyish. "Eating less junk food is so centered around what you lose ... and what we were got notification from our individuals is that health is about what you gain." The most well-known hashtag utilized by Rapid Weight Loss individuals on the organization's computerized network sheets, actually, is #NSV - or, "non-scale triumph," like fighting the temptation to eat that donut, or feeling adequate to stay aware of your children on the play area.

What's more, Oprah, the benefactor holy person of "carrying on with your best life" (and an over 8% investor in Rapid Weight Loss), likewise adulated the organization's new move in an announcement: "I have accepted that the job Rapid Weight Loss can play in individuals' lives goes a long ways past a number on the scale," she said. "As Rapid weight loss becomes Rapid Weight Loss, I accept we will keep on motivating individuals not exclusively to eat well, yet to move more, interface with others and keep on encountering the delights of a solid life."

Rapid Weight Loss is the most recent individual from the $3.7 trillion worldwide wellbeing economy going to a progressively comprehensive way to deal with keeping up a sound lifestyle to shed pounds, instead of concentrating on diet - which has for the most part comprised of making a calorie shortage by eating short of what you exercise off, or removing whole food gatherings like carbs or gluten criticized for pressing on pounds. Truth be told, the quantity of individuals saying that they are on an eating regimen dropped from 31% in 2014 to 25% in 2018, as indicated by the NPD Group, a loss of changing dispositions toward food, diet exhaustion and the body acknowledgment development advising individuals it's OK to adore their stomach cushions.

"Shoppers would prefer not to be something that is prohibitive. We don't care for eating fewer carbs," Darren Seifer, the NPD Group food utilization examiner, told Moneyish. "So in the course of the most recent decade, we're beginning to move away from 'low-this' or 'diet-that,' and beginning to grasp things that are high in protein, or probiotics that can support your body."

Furthermore, examine shows that diets don't work. An ongoing JAMA study found that individuals who concentrated on the nature of their food - eating less sugar, less refined grains and handled foods for veggies and entire foods - lost 11 to 13 pounds over a year all things considered, and without tallying calories. Then again, a 2012 investigation of in excess of 4,000 indistinguishable twins matured 16 to 25 found that the individuals who counted calories were bound to put on weight than their non-consuming less calories twins.

"The eating regimen industry has been battling with the high long haul disappointment pace of weight reduction for a long time now. As right on time as 1993, the Federal Trade Commission charged that five health improvement plans, including Rapid weight loss, made bogus and unverified cases about the adequacy of their items," Dr. Sandra Aamodt, a neuroscientist and creator of "Why Diets Make Us Fat," told Moneyish. "Numerous methodologies work for the time being, with calorie counters arriving at their least weight at around a half year in the wake of beginning an eating regimen, yet by five years after the fact, the larger part of individuals have come back to their past weight or put on weight."

The NPD Group additionally found that recent college grads and Gen-Zers expended new foods 23% more often in 2014 than individuals a similar age did only 10 years sooner. "There's a generational shift in the manner that individuals are moving toward food; crisp food has easing back become something thought of as better, and more youthful shoppers are looking for food that is not so much handled but rather more authentic," Seifer included. "It's progressively about being healthy and solid, which is a simpler method to carry on with your life in the long haul."

Dr. Aamodt concurred. "If the point of concentrating on wellbeing is to get more fit, that exertion will in all probability bomb in the long haul; however if the reason for existing is to improve wellbeing, then it's an incredible procedure," she said - in spite of the fact that the wellbeing guidance is easy to such an extent that she doesn't think individuals need to pay Rapid Weight Loss around $12 to $50 every month to get to it.

"It's uncertain that the vast majority need to pay somebody to instruct them to eat vegetables, get enough rest, and exercise for 30 minutes per day," she said. "The most significant hindrances to following this guidance will in general be basic elements, for example, absence of new produce in neighborhood stores, having no protected spot to exercise, or worry from separation or attempting to help a family with a low-paying employment. There's no application for that."

CONCLUSION

I commend you for taken this rapid weight loss freestyle guide as you have leant series of recipes to smooth your way to a wonder weight you have thought of.